Solitude, Vanity, Night

Kirsten Lodge is a Professor of Humanities and English at Midwestern State University, Texas. She translates literature from Czech and Russian. Her translations include the Decadent novel *A Gothic Soul* by Jiří Karásek ze Lvovic, *The Dedalus Book of Russian Decadence*, and Russian classics for Broadview Press.

THIS IS A SNUGGLY BOOK

Anthology and Introduction Copyright © 2008, 2025
by Kirsten Lodge.
All rights reserved.

ISBN: 978-1-64525-185-9

Solitude, Vanity, Night

An Anthology of Czech Decadent Poetry

EDITED, TRANSLATED AND WITH AN INTRODUCTION
BY **KIRSTEN LODGE**

Contents

Introduction / 7

Jiří Karásek ze Lvovic
  Miserere / 33
  Ennui / 36
  Narcosis / 38
  Tuberoses / 39
  Deathly Mood / 40
  Sleepwalker / 41
  In Memoriam / 42
  Decomposition / 43
  Metempsychosis / 44
  In Sickly Colors / 45
  Knowledge / 47
  Wafts of Dead Air / 50
  The Incubus / 53
  The Longing for Solitude / 55
  Opening Poem of the Collection *Sodom* / 57
  Venus Masculinus / 59
  Ennui / 61
  Friendship of the Soul / 63
  Io triumphe! / 66

Late Moment / 67
The Sorrow of Flesh / 69
Solitude / 70
The Deflowering of the Soul / 71
Baccanalia / 73
The Coming of the Barbarians / 76
My Poetry to the Reader / 78
The Emerald Plaque / 79
Sin / 80
Classical Triptych on Love and Song / 82

Karel Hlaváček
Preface to the Collection *In the Wee Hours* / 87
Pseudo-Japonaiserie / 89
The Vampire / 91
She Has Come / 94
I Have Tuned My Viola / 98
Anemia / 100
The Primeval Submarine Forests / 102
The Subtlety of Sorrow / 103
Vengeful Cantilena / 110

Otokar Březina
Art / 125
The Gaze of Death / 128
Apostrophe to Autumn / 130
Evening Prayer / 132
Mood / 135
Dead Youth / 136
Anniversary / 138
Scents of the Gardens of My Soul... / 140
Regret / 144

Introduction

The Historical Context

The literary movement of decadence, which is associated with the aesthetically refined and often perverse poetry of Charles Baudelaire, Paul Verlaine and Stéphane Mallarmé, achieved notoriety in France with the publication of Joris-Karl Huysmans's novel *Against Nature* (*À rebours*) in 1884. It spread quickly throughout Europe not only because its eroticism titillated readers, but also because its pessimism reflected anxieties aroused by the dissolution of traditional social and religious values. The gloomy mood of decadence found particularly fertile soil in the Czech lands, where the political climate of the mid-1890s fostered a sense of defeat and despondency. Subjects of the Austro-Hungarian Empire, the Czechs had failed to make their demands for linguistic and political equality heard through parliamentary channels, and radical measures had also come to naught. Demonstrations in Prague had led to arrests, increased censorship, and the imposition of a two-year state of emergency from 1893 to 1895. Later, in May 1897, the enactment of language ordinances allowing the use of both Czech and German for domestic governmental purposes in Bohemia led to protests and manifestations among the latter's large German population. As a result, on December 2, 1897 martial law was imposed in Prague. Economic problems further contributed to the nation's sense of frustration, which was reflected in the poetry of the Czech decadents. Although the economy was growing, it suffered from periodic crises, and poverty and poor working conditions led to the emergence of radical social movements in the last decade of the century.

Moreover, by the 1890s Czech society had become more differentiated, and national concerns no longer united the population as they had earlier in the century. The collective, once unified by nationality and religion, seemed to be disintegrating, and intellectuals continually debated the "decadence" of their society. They considered one of the chief symptoms of this "illness" of modern times to be the alienation of the individual, cut off from the communities that had provided sustenance in the past. Decadent writers self-consciously took up the themes of illness, decline, and loneliness. In contrast to conservatives who mourned the passing of the collective spirit, however, they also frequently portrayed the modern shift of emphasis from community to individual in positive terms, emphasizing the value of individualism and subjective experience. The exploration of the individual's inner world and perceptions thus became one of the fundamental tenets of the decadent movement.

The purpose of this anthology is to introduce English-speaking readers to the three most well-known Czech decadents: Jiří Karásek ze Lvovic, Karel Hlaváček, and Otokar Březina. These writers were regular contributors to the decadent journal *The Modern Revue*, founded in October 1894 by Karásek and Arnošt Procházka. Most of the poems included in this anthology were published in the mid- to late 1890s, when Czech decadence was in its heyday, though some of Karásek's poems included here were written after the turn of the century. In addition to the characteristics mentioned above—a commitment to individualism and an all-pervasive sense of futility—these poets share an obsession with the themes of exhaustion, languor, sickness, and death.

Jiří Karásek ze Lvovic (1871-1951)

Jiří Karásek was the most prolific Czech writer of decadent verse, in addition to prose, plays, and critical articles. He added the aristocratic title "ze Lvovic" ("of Lvovice") to his name after the turn of the century, claiming ancestry from the sixteenth-century astronomer and mathematician Cyprián Lvovický ze Lvovic. He thus engaged in aristocratic posing typical of decadence and, at the same time, endowed himself with the aura of an astronomer of Rudolph II's Prague, famed as a center of culture and magic. The atmosphere of Rudolph's "magic Prague" pervades many of his novels. Karásek assisted Procházka as *de facto* editor of *The Modern Revue* while working first as a postal clerk and later as the director of the Postal Museum and Archive.

In many of his poems Karásek voices the weariness of the decadent persona. However, the sickly decadent, whose prototype is the imperial subject of the late Roman Empire, longs for his opposite—the strong, healthy "barbarian." In "The Coming of the Barbarians," modeled on Verlaine's 1883 sonnet "Languor," which was considered a verse manifesto of decadence, the debauched and degenerate lyrical persona welcomes the barbarians who have come to destroy his dying civilization and build a new one on its ruins. The poem "Metempsychosis" plays a pivotal role in Karásek's poetic *oeuvre*, for here the enfeebled lyrical "I" vampirizes the barbarian. Through a transferal of psyches he thus acquires, at least temporarily, the strength and inspiration to sing out joyous pagan songs in praise of sexuality, battle, and the flaming sun, as in the declamatory verse "Io triumphe." In "Bacchanalia" he asserts that he has the strength of will to create the perfect world for himself, which will provide an antidote to unhealthy decadence. In lieu of the nuances and subtleties of the decadent aesthetic, this dream world will be full of sharp contrasts and bright colors. Primordial feelings and the sensual embrace of strong barbarian men will reinvigorate the invalid of the modern world.

The reader will note immediately that it is specifically *male* sexuality that Karásek craves. Homosexuality is a recurring theme in decadence throughout Europe, and many writers associated with the movement were homosexual. Oscar Wilde is the most famous example, and Karásek's collection of openly homosexual poetry, entitled *Sodom*, was published in response to Wilde's trials and conviction for sodomy in 1895. Karásek thus became the first Czech writer to explicitly address the subject of same-sex love. The censors confiscated

Karásek's collection immediately upon its publication, as well as the September issue of *The Modern Revue*, which had published two of the collection's most provocative homosexual poems: its opening sonnet and "Venus Masculinus." The decadent journal was continuing its battle against public opposition to homosexuality; in June 1895 it had dedicated an issue to a defense of Wilde. Karásek included many of the less objectionable poems from his confiscated collection in later books, and in 1905 he published a significantly revised, more conservative edition of *Sodom*.

What is most striking about Karásek's treatment of homosexuality is its ambivalence. Although he wishes to express his feelings of sexual longing for men with sincerity, in accordance with the decadent principle of frankness in writing about one's deepest emotions and thoughts, his poetry is at the same time imbued with a strong sense of guilt. In "Venus Masculinus" he refers to "the love that slinks like a mangy dog from night to night," and in the opening sonnet to *Sodom* the lyrical persona distances himself from the men engaging in sexual acts. Indeed, the very title of the collection evokes the concept of sin and the wrath of God. The same ambivalence characterizes *The Modern Revue*'s June 1895 defense of Wilde.

Karásek seems both to suffer beneath the weight of sin and to extol it as the ultimate expression of unbridled individuality. In "Wafts of Dead Air," the shadowy figure he meets, his alter ego, is branded by a "cursed love" for which "an unatoned guilt weighs upon his lost soul." The lyrical persona, like this phantom figure, seems doomed to exist eternally in a timeless limbo with no hope for salvation. The poem "Sin," on the other hand, joyously affirms the glory of passion, ecstasy, and disdain. Sin triumphs over the abyss, if only briefly, before collapsing into nothingness.

Given this obsession with sin, it is not surprising to find that Catholicism plays a significant role in Karásek's work. He authored numerous stories and legends about the lives of saints, monks, and nuns. Of the poems in this collection, "Misere" and "Memoriam," for instance, recall not only Baudelaire's famous poem "The Carrion," but also the Catholic baroque *memento mori* topos. They also call to mind the baroque flair for the naturalistic description, and even display, of corpses, skeletons, and decay. At the same time, Karásek was certainly trying to *épater la bourgeoisie* with his emphasis on decomposition and the "reeking, slimy beds" of corpses. The baroque *vanitas* topos is also prevalent in Karásek's work, both poetry and prose. For Karásek, in the end "all is vanity." This sentiment is clear in his 1895 poem "Spleen," in which even poetry itself is devalued. It sometimes stirs within the poet as a "final protest," but in the end it merely erupts in a "dead and useless foam." This image is comparable to Hlaváček's metaphor of poetry, or literary work in general, in the third part of "The Subtlety of Sorrow" as semen spilled by a masturbating decadent intellectual.

Karásek's ambivalence towards sexuality is reflected in oscillations between the extremes of debauchery—or at least intense desire for sex—and chastity. In "The Deflowering of the Soul," for instance, the jaded lyrical persona contends that he has crawled through all the lairs of pleasure. In "Solitude," he prays for "the embrace of hot and wild limbs," lamenting his chaste nudity, though elsewhere it is precisely solitude that he desires. Still other poems, including "Friendship of the Soul," conceive of the relationship to another man as a strong Platonic friendship between companions who are different from other people and therefore exiled from the ordinary world. Outcasts from the modern age, they participate in the spectacular collapses of Sodom, Rome, and Pompeii that so fascinated the decadents, who felt that the European culture of their own age was similarly on the brink of perdition. In contrast to these celebrations of sensuality, other poems by Karásek, such as the "Classical Triptych on Love and Song," suggest that the poet should keep all of his sensuality and emotions to himself. He should show the world an impassive, icy exterior, and channel his unsatisfied erotic feelings into his poetry. It is precisely this transformation of sexual energy into aesthetic form—strict, Parnassian form resembling a sculpture or a finely cut gem—that makes poetry beautiful, he implies. This conception of aesthetics is particularly strong in the 1905 edition of *Sodom*.

One stylistic feature that distinguishes Karásek's verse is his striking use of metaphor. "I apathetically watch the loathsome rats of thought / Scurry through the sewers of my life," he writes in one poem. Images such as these leave an indelible impression on the reader's mind. They are meant to be provocative, and their shock value demonstrates Karásek's position as a precursor of later avant-garde movements, which similarly strove to scandalize their audiences.

Karel Hlaváček (1874-98)

Many hailed Hlaváček as the most promising young decadent poet, but tuberculosis led to his untimely death in 1898. It may seem enigmatic that Hlaváček, most of whose poetry is permeated with a sense of utter hopelessness, was avidly devoted to the patriotic Sokol gymnastics movement throughout his life. Indeed, his first book of poetry, *Sokol Sonnets* (1894),[1] is dedicated entirely to the organization. However, Hlaváček's involvement with the Sokol evinces his obsession with the illness he perceived as afflicting the nation, particularly its younger generation, which he portrays as feeble and degenerate. Hlaváček's conception of the Sokol athletes parallels Karásek's vision of the barbarians: both served as idealized rejuvenating forces with the power to cure the "decadence" of society.

Hlaváček came from a working class family, and many critics have interpreted his masterpiece, the twelve-poem cycle *Vengeful Cantilena*, in the light of the unjust social conditions in the late 1890s, which he knew from personal experience. National concerns, however, are equally important in this work. The cycle depicts the failed rebellion of the Dutch and Flemish Gueux against Habsburg rule,[2] which began in 1566.

---

[1] The collection came out in December 1894, but the year 1895 is given as the date of publication in the book.

[2] Hlaváček's cycle conflates this historical event with the sixteenth-century Anabaptist rebellion in Münster as portrayed in a cycle of drawings entitled *The Anabaptists* by the German artist Josef Sattler and the watercolor *The Anabaptists* by the Czech artist Hanuš Schwaiger.

Their uprising adumbrates the Czechs' rebellion against the Habsburgs, which began in 1618 and culminated in their defeat in the 1620 Battle of White Mountain. Both rebellions were followed by merciless and devastating countermeasures. The noblemen leading the uprisings were publicly executed in 1568 and 1621, respectively, and thereafter the Habsburgs ruthlessly rooted out all opposition to their regime. The final, hopeless revolt of the destitute and starving imperial subjects in the cycle suggests a merging of contemporaneous pressing national and social issues, though the poet offers little hope of their positive resolution. The rebellion fails, and, the poet suggests fatalistically at the end of the poem, "it had to be so." Although the Dutch independence movement was eventually successful, Hlaváček gives no hint of prospective victory in the future, concluding the cycle with the memorable image of a field covered with the corpses of the defeated Gueux. The image of the suppressed revolt is common in Czech decadence. We find it, for instance, in Procházka's 1897 poem "The Crushed Revolt," Hlaváček's illustrations for the poem and the collection in which it was included (*Prostibolo duše*, which may be loosely translated as *The Painful Brothel of the Soul*[1]), and Karásek's frequent musings on the Battle of White Mountain. As in Karásek's work, the final note in Hlaváček's poetry is one of hopelessness.

Hlaváček was an artist as well as a poet, and this may be one reason why his poetry is very visual and often dreamlike. He explicitly compares his verbal art to painting—specifically to the simple and naïve, yet

---

1 *Prostibolo* is a neologism suggesting both prostitution (*prostituce*) and pain (*bolest*).

delicate and subtle art of the Japanese—in his manifesto in poetic prose, "Pseudo-Japonaiserie." Following the French symbolists, particularly Verlaine, he also gives music pride of place in his poetic *oeuvre*, both through frequent reference to musical instruments and genres—particularly ecclesiastical genres—and through euphonic assonances and other poetic harmonies.

In another manifesto in poetic prose, the preface to his first decadent collection, *In the Wee Hours*, Hlaváček states that his task is "to capture everything sublime, mysterious, anemic and timorous in delicate mystifications." The five adjectives in this definition are among Hlaváček's favorite words. He is attracted to anything that is beautiful and enigmatic, yet pale, sickly, shy, and fragile. It is also important to note that his poems are often "mystifications"—that is, he is not entirely serious, but rather plays with the conventions of decadence, boldly challenging and often baffling the reader, and frequently undercutting the literal meaning of his work with irony.

Karásek offers another insightful characterization of Hlaváček's aesthetics: "Instead of light he loves reflections; instead of sharp colors, their mere shade; instead of proximity, distance; instead of the present, the past and bygone days; instead of experience, longing; and instead of life, death" (*Impresionisté* 100).[1] Hlaváček favors the diffuse light of the moon, shadows, fog, and nuances. Suggestion, as opposed to straightforward naming, is one of his fundamental aesthetic principles, as it was for Mallarmé. He strives primarily to evoke a

---

1 This article was originally published in *The Modern Revue* in June 1898.

mood through his poetry, generally one of melancholy and yearning.

In the programmatic poem "The Vampire" Hlaváček proclaims that the vampire is "the symbol of decadence." Here the "noble madman" soaring through the skies is a symbol of inspiration—specifically, decadent inspiration, as he is a disdainful lover of all that is sick and feeble. With his "sticky, rough tongue," Hlaváček's vampire is also an emblem of degeneracy, or regression to earlier stages of evolutionary development. He spreads contagion to his victims, poisoning the admiring lyrical persona himself. The narrator, like the vampire, acquires the sublime freedom necessary to soar through the realms of decadent inspiration, though he must pay for this liberation with his physical health. Karásek similarly describes the power of decadence to infect the reader with its themes—"solitude, vanity, night"—in the poem "My Poetry to the Reader," which provides the title of this collection. Hlaváček's vampire may be read as congruous with Karásek's vampires in another way as well: although Hlaváček is not known to have been homosexual,[1] the fact that the vampire's other

---

[1] Karásek, though, suggests in his memoirs that Hlaváček had same-sex desires. When he asked Hlaváček why he was so enthusiastic about the Sokol movement, Karásek writes, Hlaváček responded that he was searching for a close friend, which he believed to have found in the gymnast Karel Hron. Karásek narrates Hlaváček's story as follows: "[...] He would go to the Karlin Sokol gym with a pounding heart to see the beautiful champion Hron there. His body, he said, was as ideal as that of a fighter in antiquity. He said that a more perfect body did not exist and that he yearned to have Hron for a friend. And Hron, he said, broke his neck one evening while training at the Sokolovna. He was dead. [...] he liked Hron so much, that after his death he began to date his girlfriend

escapades described in the poem are erotic may imply an undertone of homosexuality in his relationship with the narrator, who must have engaged in similar contact with him to have been infected with vampirism. This interpretation is supported by the fact that Hlaváček certainly knew Karásek's numerous previously published poems containing the vampirism topos, including "Metempsychosis" and "The Incubus," in which it has marked homosexual connotations.

Like Karásek, Hlaváček is obsessed with the idea of sin. For the Czech decadents, as for decadents throughout Europe, individuals are tainted not only by their own crimes and debauchery, but also by the sins they have inherited from their ancestors. This is particularly true if they are noblemen. Indeed, one of the foremost clichés of decadence is the "last scion of a noble line" motif. Des Esseintes, the protagonist of Huysmans's *Against Nature*, is the most famous example of this character type. The typical "last scion" must above all be sickly, suffering from nervous illnesses and, frequently, syphilis. He often ends up mad, like the protagonist of Karásek's 1900 novel *A Gothic Soul*. He is usually sated with an immoderate, lecherous lifestyle (particularly in Western decadence) and has retreated into solitude, usually at a large family estate or castle, where he creates a world in accordance with his elitist aesthetic whims. He is pessimistic and misanthropic, and he is burdened with all of the guilt of his ancestors. Hlaváček's poetry is filled with figures such as these. His

---

[...]." Karásek's testimony, however, is most likely colored by his own homosexuality and should not be taken at face value without additional evidence.

vampire, for instance, "the last scion of once-powerful ducal lines", is hopelessly degenerate, as he lives not from fresh blood, but from "virginal juices / infected with hereditary atrophy." Knowing he is destined to be the last representative of his noble family, the lyrical voice of "She Has Come," "heir of all the weaknesses of [his] impotent line," barricades himself in his castle as he waits for death. Finally, the decadent protagonist of "The Subtlety of Sorrow" is described as "vampiric," for he has inherited the syphilis that caused his father's insanity. Karásek too thematizes the motif of inherited sin. In the 1895 poem "Spleen" he stylizes himself as the last scion of a distinguished line who has inherited all of his ancestors' ailments, which, he suggests, are related to their erotic passions—i.e., he is suffering from inherited syphilis.

Otokar Březina (1868-1929)

Otokar Březina was the pseudonym of Václav Jebavý, who worked as a provincial schoolteacher. His later poetry is generally more optimistic, but his first collections, especially *Mysterious Distances* of 1895, manifest typically decadent characteristics such as pessimism, doubt, and an obsession with suffering, death, and suicide. Whereas Karásek yearned for civilization's rejuvenation by barbarians and Hlaváček promoted the Sokol, Březina increasingly placed his faith in a mystical elite brotherhood of brilliant minds, both living and dead, who, he believed, would join forces and miraculously transfigure the fallen world. After the turn of the century Březina shifted his focus from poetry to poetic essays similar to those of the Belgian symbolist Maurice Maeterlinck.

Březina's poetry is immediately distinguishable from that of Hlaváček and Karásek. Unlike their work, it is cosmic, sparkling with radiance sharply contrasted with darkness and sweltering with heat juxtaposed to icy cold. Its imagery encompasses the depths of caverns beneath the earth, its frozen poles, and the stars in the heavens. His poetic persona, like the poet himself, reels from desperation to ecstasy. Březina's syntax is extremely complex and demands that the reader unravel it. As a result, on first reading emotional intonation and the texture of the words dominate over semantics, and subsequent readings demand intellectual engagement with the text.

Březina has a predilection for oxymoron and paradox. He uses phrases such as "the flight of dead butterflies" and "the shimmer of extinguished colors," which he uses to create the effect of "beautiful nothingness"—metaphors over a void that can exist only in poetry. These phrases denoting things that cannot exist in reality often describe the persona's inner world, which is thus portrayed as something mysterious, unstable, and irrational. "Scents of the Gardens of My Soul" explores the traces of past memories in depth through their metaphoric fragrances. The lyrical voice shifts from nostalgia to grief, breaking into semi-coherent rapturous exaltation towards the poem's end, only to conclude on a note of anguish. The soul of the decadent persona is the polar opposite of the stable, knowable subject of positivism, against which the decadents rebelled. This revolt against reason led them to explore the subconscious, which is prominent in much of Hlaváček's poetry, and the mystical, which pervades Březina's work. Both of these poets at times transcend reason, breaking into emotional streams of imagery not connected by logic, as at the end of Hlaváček's "She Has Come" and in the second stanza of Březina's "Regret," as well as in the raving climax of his "Scents of the Gardens of My Soul."

In Březina's programmatic poem "Art," art is promoted as a mystical cult embracing the shades of great artists as well as living new initiates. Art is thus closely affiliated with the death. In "The Gaze of Death" Březina describes his initiation into art as a fascination with death. He must summon the courage to follow death in order to fathom its mysteries. In both poems, however, the persona feels he is too weak to undertake the monumental task of initiation into the mystical realm of the Unknown beyond life that is necessary for artistic greatness, and he anticipates his ultimate fatal collapse, "like a defeated priest," at the altars of the deity of Art. He longs for transcendence and is prepared to sacrifice everything to it, though he knows from the outset that he is doomed to failure, like Hlaváček's Gueux. Nevertheless, he prays to the mystical deity of Art, begging for suffering and pain, which he feels are essential prerequisites to creation, and he promises to sacrifice the sensual pleasures of life in the name of the supreme ideal. In "Art" Březina merges the decadent conception of Art as a cult propagated by Mallarmé with decadent imagery—morbid descriptions of the mystical cemetery, suffering, and death, and an erotic description of the pleasures he is willing to give up in the name of his ideal. He also employs imagery from the Catholic liturgy, detached from Church doctrine. With its elaborate, solemn rituals in magnificent cathedrals, its emphasis on the irrational and mysterious, and its morbid taste for suffering, Catholicism attracted many Western decadent writers as well, including Huysmans, Verlaine, and Wilde.

The longing for death is reiterated in most of Březina's poems included here. In "Scents of the Garden of My Soul," death is a cool breeze "from the shores of silent rivers that flow into the bays of Death" that refreshes the lyrical persona on an unbearably hot day. "Mood" evokes a similar sultry, oppressive day, culminating in suicide. "Evening Prayer" is especially notable as an extended eulogy of death, conceived as a mystical revelation of all of the mysteries of the cosmos. In "Dead Youth," it is not a human being who has died, but the time of the persona's youth. He senses that he has not taken advantage of it or gained any pleasure from it, and he feels as guilty for its "death" as a lover would feel for the suicide of a maiden he had seduced. As he often does, Březina saves this striking image for the poem's final line. The theme of the persona's life wasted without any positive experience, especially love, recurs in many of Březina's early poems.

In "Apostrophe to Autumn" the desire for death is metaphorically merged with the season of dying, autumn. Bright red and golden leaves are falling, and fruit is overripe, near putrefaction. The leaves seem to be made of gold, i.e., the natural appears to be artificial, crafted by human hands. This is another common trope of decadence, which worships the artificial as superior to the natural, a preference that is reflected in Březina's self-consciously opulent language. This poem also illustrates Březina's fondness for the apostrophe, which he shares with Karásek. Thus, although Březina is often considered more of a symbolist than a decadent poet, at least in his early work he has much in common with Karásek and Hlaváček. Above all, the three poets share a sense of utter futility and despair, which is frequently expressed in Březina's poetry as a yearning for death and a striving for transcendence that he knows is doomed to failure.

A Decadence of Hunger

In a letter of 1893, Březina wrote that he had decided to become a decadent, "a poet of those souls that are disappointed and satiated *with their own hunger*, as I am, a poet of overly excited, sensitive nerves, pale bodies, without strength, hope and muscles" (*Korespondence* 277; my emphasis). The phrase "with their own hunger" is of paramount importance here, because metaphorical hunger is what distinguishes Czech decadence from its Western counterpart. Like the Czechs, the French expressed pessimism and a conviction that their generation was feeble and neurasthenic. Their decadent characters were also satiated, but they were sated from excess, and they sought ever new sensations to satisfy their jaded sensibilities. The Czechs, on the other hand, conceived of themselves as "hungry," and they embraced decadence as an expression of their want and their weariness. Above all, they were tired of waiting in vain for political and linguistic equality. Moreover, while the French had a formidable cultural tradition in relation to which poets could purport to be "decadent," the Czechs enjoyed a relatively modest tradition. In addition, their perception of their cultural greatness had recently been undermined by the revelation in the 1880s that the Zelenohorský and Královédvorský manuscripts, until then believed to be artifacts of the thirteenth and tenth centuries, respectively, were early nineteenth-century forgeries. The Czechs thus felt themselves to be in a cultural and political vacuum, and it was the pessimism and futility of decadence that attracted them more than its themes of overripeness, indulgence, and excess. As many observers from the 1890s through the present day have noted,[1] Czech decadence is a "decadence of hunger" rather than a decadence of satiation. This is why so many Czech decadent personae are drained, bloodless, and anemic, and it explains why we find so many vampires in Czech decadent poetry, insatiably lusting for fresh blood.

A Note on the Translations

These three poets frequently used strict metrical and rhyme schemes, and they strove for musicality in their verse. It is difficult, of course, to preserve such finely wrought poetry in translation. I have endeavored to

---

[1] These commentators include František X. Krejčí, writing in the 1890s, and the later critics Fedor Soldan and Robert Pynsent.

preserve an imprint of each poem's original form as much as possible, loosening it as necessary. Thus if a quatrain has an *abab* rhyme scheme, for instance, I will generally not rhyme the first and third lines, but will use rhyme or, more frequently, alliteration or assonance in the second and fourth lines. Because I feel the form of the poem is often more important than its literal meaning, I sometimes slightly alter its semantics, as little as possible, to capture the necessary alliteration. My approach to the poems' sound structure and rhythm is analogous: I attempt to convey these formal aspects in translation, though more loosely than in the original Czech. All three poets represented here also authored unrhymed poetry and poetic prose, examples of which are included in this collection.

Acknowledgements

I am profoundly grateful to Chris Harwood for painstakingly comparing all of my translations with the originals and making numerous helpful suggestions. I incorporated into the final versions many words, phrases and, in a few cases, even entire lines that he proposed. I am indebted to Chris for his invaluable comments on my introduction as well. I would also like to thank Libuše Heczková for her support. Without her encouragement and vision, this project may never have been realized. Of course, I am fully responsible for any inadequacies remaining in the anthology.

Works Cited

Březina, Otokar. *Korespondence I (1884-1908)*. Brno: Host, 2004.

Karásek ze Lvovic, Jiří. *Impressionisté a ironikové: Dokumenty k psychologii literární generace let devadesátých. Kritické studie*. Praha: Symposion, 1903.

Karásek, Jiří. *Vzpomínky*, ed. Gabriela Dupačová and Aleš Zach. Prague: Thyrsus, 1994.

Sources of the Original Poems

For each poem I have provided the date of its original publication as part of a collection.[1] The English titles of the collections from which the poems included here were drawn are as follows:

Březina, Otokar. *Mysterious Distances*, 1895; *Light in the West*, 1896.

Hlaváček, Karel. *In the Wee Hours*, 1896; *Vengeful Cantilena*, 1898.

Karásek ze Lvovic, Jiří. *Walled-Up Windows*, 1894; *Sodom*, 1895; *The Aristocratic Book*, 1896; *Sexus Necans: The Pagan Book*, 1897; *Sodom*, 1905.

---

1 Where Karásek provides the exact date on which the poem was written, I have given that date instead.

I used the following sources for the translations in this anthology:

Březina, Otokar. *Spisy* I-III. Praha: Česká akademie věd a umění, 1933-39.

Hlaváček, Karel. *Dílo I-III*. Praha: Kvasnička a Hampl, 1930.

Karásek ze Lvovic, Jiří. *Básně z konce století*. Praha: Thyrsus, 1995.

Karásek ze Lvovic, Jiří. *Sodoma*. Praha: Mladá fronta, 2002.

Solitude, Vanity, Night

Jiří Karásek ze Lvovic

Miserere

O dead of the graveyards, watched by the moon's
   radiance
that trembles as though drunk on the pallor of lilies,
you, decaying in the darkness of crypts shining white,
as a haze lightly mists around them, fine and silvery,

you, rotting in corners amidst sunken tombs
where the green of rotten trunks shimmers,
your ghastly procession in the mirrors of my soul,
veiled, shivers like a nebulous chain of images

imagined, that vanish once they're touched,
as the down of fallen snow melts in a thaw,
like the shiny reflection of unclear images
in the mirrors of lakes quicksilvered in the fog.

O mysterious shades, wandering the quiet night,
O dead in shrouds and heavy silks
that rustle rottenly and stink of corpses,
you, with Mystery on your decaying lips,
your soul returns to your reeking, slimy beds,
benumbed and heavy with oppressive sleep,

to extinguished eyes, and into those empty hollows,
seeking an obscure phantom, it is lost in sudden ecstasy.

It wants to find the thoughts whose reflections
   sparkled there,
it wants to divine the past dreams of your spirit,
it wants to find the extinguished glow that once lit up
   your eyes,
it wants to find the salty heat that dried your tears.

It wants to immerse itself in everything again, to see to
   the very bottom,
even that which defies its inquiring gaze,
but only the jeer of those hollows stares back at it,
and the emptiness of the skull, from which all of the
   hair has decayed.

O dead youth, where are the passions that, in the time
   of love,
nervously played that mad melody
on the strings of your nerves, ardent to stifling
   faintness?—
I see only white bones, and a grimace and laughter in
   your teeth.

O dead lady, where is the smile of your lips,
where is your hair, saturated in the heady
scent of violets, where is the grace of your limbs, to
   your lover a gift?—
I see only white bones, and a grimace and laughter in
   your teeth.
O my father, my brother—all of you I hold dear,

decaying nearby and in distant cemeteries—
where is the glow of your eyes, where are the potent
    springs of your love?—
I see only white bones, and a grimace and laughter in
    your teeth.

Oh, sing, my song, woven into a funeral shroud,
like a faded rose in rotten silk,
sing a mourning verse, heavy as a death knell,
like an iron lament, for all of the dead, sing pity:

sing love for all of the souls who lived without
    compassion,
tormented by pain, sated with tears and sighs,
sing to the haggard souls wandering in the blue lights
now in the old graveyards, in the mystical nights.

1893

Ennui

Day drags after drowsy day,
as when hooded monks walk through passageways
    from their cells—
a thickened gloom in which colors are extinguished
suffuses everything, so the eye cannot tell
where the slate sky is, where the gray earth is,
where the curve of the horizon is, dim and pallid,
everything rains ash and mingles and washes out
in that deceptive light that is so like shadow,
and the eye stares only into emptiness and dense smoke,
and thick clouds that smell of pewter, damp and black.

The soul longs to be scorched by heat, then it longs to
    get drunk on darkness,
it yearns now for day, now for night,
steps resound in the empty chamber where weariness
    creeps—
and in the end everything is tedious in that misty light
and that rain of ash and grief as though somebody had
    died,
in that gloom without contours and sharp lines,
without bright colors and varied tints,

where in slinking shadows everything lengthens and
   quivers.
And the weary soul merges with the sorrow of everything.

1893

Narcosis

The herbs' bitter green has paled into a sickly white,
the colorful blossoms have dried into a glassy hue.
After the sun's intense heat its lustrous rays,
as if encrusted with lime, shine dully through

in the sky, aflame with a washed-out blue.
And in the boredom of busy streets
trembles the heavy air, full of miasmas and stink,
in which, as from red-hot furnaces, lazily drifts the heat.

Everything is dead. On the window panes
that flame blue, in hard vibrations
the buzzing of flies whirs on, long and agitated.
And drugged, senseless, and faint,
I feel bitter dust on my lips, fire on my brain,
and, in my entire body, a weight, a weight...

1893

Tuberoses

> *...and our death comes on,*
> *holy and calm as the night.*
> Moore

In the languorous scent of tuberoses, breathing oblivion,
in the final night that will see no morning,
my soul shall depart into an endless sleep,
as though rocked by the beat of angels' wings.

In the languorous scent of tuberoses, breathing oblivion,
my unfulfilled longings and hopes shall be consoled,
and shall follow like a shadow, like an unfinished dream,
behind the shadow of my soul.

1893

Deathly Mood

My soul is a gloomy vaulted cellar
where spider webs envelop every niche.
The breath of mold and dust waft here, and light
strays in but rarely, fearful, pale and sick.

My soul is a vaulted cellar where only
old things are cast to slowly putrefy.
A gray shadow lurks there, long and silent,
and sometimes sighs in the oppressive, deathly quiet.

1893

Sleepwalker

Like a mystical and holy white rose,
the moon glows in the black drapery of night,
and my soul, overcome by neuroses,
full of longing, drowns itself in its light.

Ever paler, it bears the reflection of faded gold
and the color of lilies in gardens that pine,
that mystical moon, that holy moon,
that glows in the black drapery of night.

In vain do I hide my eyes in pillows' snow,
my soul is again overcome by the magic of dead charms,
and enfeebled, it drowns itself in the light of the moon,
like a mystical and holy rose,
streaming into the black drapery of night.

1893

In Memoriam

Your soft, damp hair, my friend,
now in the frightful grave slowly, slowly rots,
and the decayed, disintegrating shroud
conceals your repulsive, decomposing body.

That body full of strength and joy,
those eyes, like your dreamy soul, full of promise,
that hair, intensely fragrant,
in the grave all of you slowly, slowly rots.

And it seems to me that the same loathsome worm
now burrows into my own body,
that Death clads me in the same disintegrating shroud,
and that already my own hair now, my friend,
like yours, slowly, slowly rots...

1893

Decomposition

The sun's shield melts into bronze,
in the sickly air its glow is smothered.
The air thickens, pallid and ashen,
above a land choked by the stench of lime dust.

Everything is parched: even the sated green of the grass,
spattered by the brush of Spring in the distant ravine,
and the sharp sand, which grates so harshly
to the rhythm of my steps, and wearies me.

And the smell of rot is everywhere,
Decay spills out its putrefying poisons generously,
and even the sun, so strangely red, is rotting...
In my veins hot blood evaporates,
and my body, weakening, awaits the end
of agony, and the end of all things.

1893

Metempsychosis

I don't know who you were. But it often seems to me,
In sudden apprehension that flashes like a sword
Bared in the sun:
I saw you once amidst barbaric carnage,
Amidst the clash of weapons and in fire and blood,
Amidst the canter of neighing horses I glimpsed you.

In steel armor, on an untamed horse,
Like a whirlwind you rushed forth, your shield upraised,
Your metal shield, in the din,
You pierced my white body with your spear
And cried out brutally, inebriated by your win,
Blinded and deafened, you brutally cried out.

A wild, cursed pleasure intoxicates me,
Furious lust now whips my passion on:
To rush forth, to throw myself on your body,
On your hot and sensual body,
To suck all of your blood from your lips,
To stifle the breath in your throat,
To break your bones and rip apart your flesh,
Your swarthy, cruel, barbarian flesh.

1894

In Sickly Colors

As languorous music would respire through the land,
Auguring winter frosts, in the winds' sharp plaint,
In the yellow of timorous lights and the scarlet of
    fallen leaves
That bleed along the road in diffuse and spreading stains,

My soul too is deadened and subdued,
Like those sickly hues of rotting and decay,
And it festers in the cold and stagnant air
Of dank and empty gardens, as silent as the grave.

My soul is redolent of loneliness and pungent cold,
In the breath of speechless mornings merged with dew,
Of the weight of dusks in which all is submerged,
Of the melancholy of dark and hidden pools.

It moves from void to void like a shyly passing shade,
In turbid apathy it wanders without aim
To the befouled horizon that envelops it in filth,
It no longer yearns for anything, lazy even for disdain.
And only sometimes does it seem that something sighs,
Somewhere in the voiceless depths, in hidden pain,

Where the silent scent would lie as though interred,
With the play of subtle hues and bright colors' fervid
    flame,
That something stirs to life in those unfathomed depths,
In a secret trembling, like an unfulfilled hope,
That in a final protest something still ferments,
Which will soon erupt in a dead and useless foam.

1895

Knowledge

> *Je l'aime pour ta douleur* [1]
> Péladan

You who have the soul of the one who sought me in past lives. In the trembling of your hand I feel the intimacy and favor I gained so long ago.

Like a fragrance that is too pervasive, you have filled the chamber of my soul. You have revived and dispersed its sorrows as a white wedding procession disperses the mournful shadows of an old cathedral.

Your smile is like a flowing veil of mourning crape cast onto a dead face. Your voice is muffled and subdued, like drumbeats at funerals of murdered regents.

Shall we merge together in gloomy, unlit streets where illustrious ages have hung out their silence, just as we did back then, when we wasted our youth, two monks over ancient parchments, two pallid faces like moons over the colorful miracles of the missals?

---
1 I love him because it hurts you.

Exiles in times of petty commercialism and filth, born for centuries of glory, we shall join our souls in a single rhythm, we shall mingle our bodies in a brotherhood of blood.

Or, contemporaries of Plato, intoxicated by kisses and the friendship of our souls, we shall listen to the wisdom of sweet lips late into the night after a feast at Agathon's house, amidst the bodies of our friends, fast asleep after heady wine.

We shall fight in the sacred armies of Thebes, two lovers amidst bloody carnage. And as we fall on our shields to enemy blows, our fraternal limbs shall commingle, and our blood shall pour out into a single drink, which our lips shall drink at the hour of death.

Inhabitants of Pompeii, with roses in our hair, on the way to the games when the unbridled elements overtake us with death, we will display smiles of a joy that mortals have never known to the sons of the late century who dig out our bodies.

Oversensitive Romans, an exhausted race, in chambers where the languor of perfumes lingers, in our kisses we will bury our premonitions of the barbarians, approaching the city gates in wild hordes.

At the court of Alexander, the pope of harlots, two sorrowful pages, we shall wander amidst the orgies as a bare foot stomps with contempt on a tiara and the pope falls asleep on shameless breasts, and we shall hearken to funeral laments resounding in the distance as a muted reminder of death!

Sons of Sodom, we shall watch fire rain down upon our roofs. And perishing in the flames, we shall press close to one another in a frenzy of passion, and we shall bare our limbs to the pleasures of love, disdaining Jehovah and laughing at His wrath...

Nuremberg, July 1895

Wafts of Dead Air

> *Mainte image se perd en la lumière neuve.*[1]
> Ghil

Wafts of dead air fall into my silence like withered leaves into a mute hollow. Presence distances itself from me now, and my soul is full of confusion and languor, as though a long illness had drained all of my strength.

Like a sphinx half buried in sand, I rise up from the past. I come from times that no longer exist, and in my dead gaze shine suns that were not created for my eyes...

Shadowy images like exhausted figures stagger through my head. Sterile thoughts are resurrected there and die, as vain as the black surfaces of mirrors hanging in darkness.

Long decayed layers of remote times come to life in my soul. A mysterious hand has touched them, and the decomposed fragrance that had been blown away returns with the color that had perished in mold.

---

1 Many an image is lost in the new light.

Like shadows on a white wall, formless thoughts traverse my consciousness. And my soul follows them like a reflection behind a nocturnal boat on which a light has been lit.

It seems to me that I am living the dream of an indistinct life that was once true. The dream of a life there, somewhere below, immeasurably far below, where my memory drops now like a plumb-line into the ocean depths without reaching the bottom.

I have visions of a shadow who walks past me, then returns and walks towards me. And it seems to me that I recognize who it is who has crossed my path.

I tremble with longing, as rotten leaves tremble beneath a sudden gust of wind, leaves hanging over a dead lake, in oblivion and deep sleep.

But the shadow is silent and keeps his distance. I want to stop him, but the silence kills my cry. The silence of distances and age, hanging extinguished like a lifeless, rigid mask, in the deathliness of everything, compressed by space.

But the shadow returns, and he is different. I sense, though, that it is he who sought me before. He now has the countenance of a new life, but his soul is the same as before.

He stares long and fixedly into my eyes and does not retreat into the gloom. It seems that an unexpressed reproach trembles in his gaze, and an unatoned guilt weighs upon his lost soul.

The mark of sin stains his brow. And the damp traces of a cursed love seem still to linger on his trembling lips. Beneath his long vesture his body seems to undulate as though in the spasms of a perverse passion.

Everything comes back: the dream sinks into the indistinct twilight, the inaudible coulisse into the trapdoor of Time. I alone remain, motionless, rigid, amidst the change of everything.

Like a sphinx half buried in sand, I rise up from the past. I come from times that no longer exist, and in my dead gaze shine suns that were not created for my eyes...

1895

The Incubus

> *Qualis nox fuit illa, Di Deaeque!*
> *Quam mollis torus! Haesimus calentes,*
> *Et transfudimus hinc et hinc labellis*
> *Errantes animas! Valete curae*
> *Mortales: ego sic perire coepi!*[1]
> Petronius, Satiricon LXXIX

O unused nakedness of white limbs, icy, shivering,
How often has fire suddenly inflamed you, in the first
    swoon of sleep,
And the weight of a sweet body descended upon your
    virgin lap from afar,
—In vain! Only longing has trembled in the air, like
    the plaint of phtisical violins!

I am drifting off to sleep. He comes. He is beautiful,
    but dark. Lover,

---

1 Ye gods and goddesses! O what a night! / The bed, so soft! Our souls had lost / Their way—we lay so warm and tight— / Goodbye, care. I've said my last goodnight. Petronius, *The Satyricon and The Fragments*, trans. J. P. Sullivan. New York: Penguin, 1971, 89.

Shade of the Abyss, whom I have summoned, having
    died to the world,
I was conceived for this one hour, predestined for you,
I see the pleasure for which I have prayed tremble on
    the bloody flower of your lips!

I am dying! Do you not sense it? The ardor of your
    embrace consumes me,
And your fierce kisses drive me mad! Are you leaving?
    I tremble
With fear and longing, staring into the black fire of
    your demonic eyes.
O Solitude! By midnight, when the lamp burns out,
    you will find me cold on my bed,
And, like a lost foreigner, in vain will your brother,
    Sadness, knock
At the black doors of the dead house of my soul...

                      February 20, 1895, midnight

The Longing for Solitude

An acrid, bitter poison has poured through me,
and with it waft clouds of black incense, thickened,
    silently,
and only from far away, as from a saint's palms,
breathes that longing for whiteness, languorously pure
    in dying.

That longing for whiteness that suggests from a distance,
as in the rhythm of anticipated, invisible waves
that die in mists whose constant sway of weariness
leads, with the same music, into the giddiness of
    dreams full of plaints.

And wounded by life and inundated with the same gray
that harshly cuts its frigid tones in a cruel and hopeless
    game
into the rainbow, splendor, and luminosity of dreams,
like a lost sailor, nostalgically, again I dream:

that my soul will rebuild a cathedral for itself
of that proud Solitude, which it had contemptuously
    laid waste,

where the lights of memories burn in the old gold of
    lamps,
pouring the play of brilliance into the crypts of dead days,
of that proud Solitude where all is forgotten,
where all that wearies and sickens the spirit is assuaged,
as soothed rhythms of water sleep somewhere in a cove,
rent in the distance by the defiance of cliffs, and the
    shock of waves.

                                            1895

Opening Poem of the Collection *Sodom*

> *the men, giving up natural intercourse with women,*
> *were consumed with passion for one another...*[1]
> Rom. 1: 27

Exhausted race, lounging in stifling beds with distaste,
Sapped members that glutted nakedness no longer lures.
To clamorous orgies! May flames burn the roofs on the morrow,
Tonight we will blaze, carouse, laugh, and shout!
Harlot, undress!

Outside it's oppressive, the sky apathetically gleams.
The copper moon heavily, sullenly melts into red.
The air reeks of plague, men feebly plod through the streets,
Palish lampoons of humanity in palaces' unfeeling shade.

But inside, in the redolent darkness of bedrooms, all
   have gone mad.

---

[1] *The New Oxford Annotated Bible*. New York: Oxford University Press, 1994.

A furious lust drives man to man.
All is vanity! Perversion has long lost its savor and juice!

The night finds nude men in men's arms,
Unsated, asleep. Jehovah! You made us too vile!
Life is repulsive, and death is banal!

1895

Venus Masculinus

On Your altar they do not lay fragrant roses, joyful as
 virgins' smiles,
As a choir sings, and people bow down to the temple
 floor in clouds of incense.
Your altar is cold, frigid, and only on dank, moldy nights
Does a lone lover furtively steal in to kiss Your robes.

In the empty temple, sullied with mud and spit,
Before a rigid, mute god, disdained by the crowd,
He lays black scabious, the gift of a passion scorned
 and cursed,
A sacrifice to the love that slinks like a mangy dog
 from night to night.

"God of the love of men!" weary lips whisper in vain
 prayer.
My longing summons You and seeks You, as a night
 butterfly
Seeks the toxic scent of black blossoms that will kill it.

—But from dark holes stare unfeeling, empty eyes at this ecstatic invocation.
The god is dead, and his green body reeks of plague.
Do you not hear the laughter? It is nature, mocking her own creation!

1895

Ennui

Everything hangs wearily, as though oppressed by an
 invisible weight.
Vain nights tremble over a bed on which sleep shall
 never descend.
Gray, extinguished days look into the ennui of a
 solitary soul,
Like ghastly, importunate blind men waiting for alms.

Like funeral processions to the gates of old graveyards,
Sorrowful thoughts, like veiled women in mourning, enter
The solitary soul. They walk hesitantly and silently,
Like those who gather for a sudden funeral on their
expected wedding day...

Dauphin of an old, distinguished line, its last, late scion,
I have all the ailments of my ancestors and for all of
 their passions,
Feeble, drained, bloodless, I stagger like a ghost
 through the rooms
Where they stored the trophies of their military glory
 and portraits of the women they'd loved.

And I approach the mirror and examine in it my traits:
I have the sickly beauty of those ordained to die,
Who will perish slowly like the broken stems of white
 flowers in hothouses.

Cries of pleasure, destined for others, leave me
 indifferent.
I have outlived the dead by a few seconds, and in the
 midst of an alienated world,
I fix my listless eyes on a sun that was not created for
 my languor.

1895

Friendship of the Soul

You who have joined me to walk through the noisy streets of life, my friend, whose reveries have diffused their fragrance into the proud solitude of my days, I wish to sing out my ardent favor towards Your soul in the colors of my Song, and, in the undulations of music, in the rhythms of melancholy verses, say to You: brother!

Roses do not blossom for us in the earthly garden where others gather them. Pleasures do not invite us to the halls where banquets are prepared for others. We walk alone, with veils of mist before our eyes, following our own mysterious sun, like those intoxicated by a fragrance that spurts out of Muscat grapes and pours forth from mint.

Shadows fall on our paths as from black flags hung out on the day of a funeral. In the ports of our souls venturous ships from expeditions long past slowly rot... And the longings that weep in our souls like ailing violins fan us with the mysterious trembling of endlessly dispersed cosmic sorrow.

Exiles in the muddy street of today, beneath a sky clouded with filthy smoke, we who were born for white days of glory and the glowing colors of delicate harmony, we carry in our souls the beauty of lines and smiles that blossom on pale faces, and when scorn wants to wound us, we dream of the marble beauty of palaces.

And we dream of a bright, sunny sky shining with blue and gold, of sacred groves with the proud nakedness of slender, erect gods, and our dreams go off into the distance like a procession of pilgrims towards a sacred finger, and our thoughts go with them like weary clouds behind a flock of white birds.

My dearest, I want to sing a Triumphant Hymn in a flow of fulminating notes, I want to pour out the finest perfumes and ointments on Your serene name, I want to burn in the lamp of Your memory, an impatiently flaring flame, I want to swoon in the garden of Your soul, a damp flower dipped in blood!

In the fire of Your longing I want to burn up the bitter disappointments of life, in the rain of Your falling flowers I want to stifle the tedium of my days, into the heart of Your being I want to cast the green shine of my soul's anticipation, which, polarized, is refracted from the atmosphere of the Unknown.

I want to flare up in colors through the prism of Your soul, I want to quake in Your sight with a sick silver longing for Light, and, consumed by Your love, I want to sing a Triumphant Hymn in a flow of fulminating notes, and, in the ardent rhythms of my Song, say to You: friend—brother!

1896

Io triumphe!

Roman trombone fanfares at the head of the procession!
And the sun in flames with its fiery breath
Makes everything blaze: the booty of statues and gold vessels,
And peacocks of simoom and victory plaques.

O proud masculinity of bodies on rearing stallions,
Staining the earth with lather... In the colony
The sun tanned them, their nakedness,
As dark as bronze... Io triumphe!

Ferocity rises into all of my nerves.
A stream of violent passions penetrates my bones.
The frenzy of battle beats into my muscles.

I spur on restive barbarian rhythms like a steed,
And, a pagan poet, I proudly cast into verse
Blood, colors, bronze and the sun in flames!

1897

Late Moment

I know, that moment will come: in the midst of empty
  darkness,
You shall forget about the twilight of everything, and
  in my lap
You shall lay your heavy head, with no memory of the
  past,
And we shall celebrate the sabbath of our late and
  doubting love...

We shall not think of the rosy ennui of the skies after
  sunset!
We shall forget that we survived Sodom and lived
  through the destruction of Pompeii!
We shall forget all of our past sins and burnt-out
  pleasures,
You, indifferent to all, and I, moved by the sorrows I
  have endured.

I shall lower my head to you and, trembling, I shall
  embrace
Your ruined being in the silence pregnant with unease,
And I shall drink in your soul with eyes in which
  horror will grow cold...

And as you burrow your heavy head in dull spasm in
 my lap,
I shall sing you a mad lullaby about those who come late,
And, with no memory of the past, long for the sabbath
 of their desperate love!

1897

The Sorrow of Flesh

> —*Hypocrite lecteur,—mon semblable,—mon frère*
> Baudelaire[1]

Into ravings of emptiness, into delusive reveries of silence,
Delirious from opium and stupefied by passion,
For the soothing death of my soul I called you,
A poet deathly tired from life and ennui.

O vain fever and vain tremor of longing!
Today I feel: Your hot flesh is languid,
It is dreadfully languid, it is deathly weary,
Your drained flesh, your wilted flesh.

In vain I warmed your lap with the heat of my youth,
In vain I bathed your lips with kisses!
Others had already drunk that chalice to the last drop...

The heat of other bodies had consumed the nakedness
    of your limbs,
And if, unexpectedly, I were to enter your soul now,
I would find there the disgust of all who preceded me...

1897

---
[1] Hypocritical reader—my semblance—my brother.

Solitude

You who heat the polar night of my soul,
O sensual longing! I feel: You tremble in my pale body.
In the hours of Shadow I approach your deceptive mirror.
Nakedness chills me, white nakedness, chaste nakedness...

O you eyes, so deep, like mysterious smiling in an
    obscure dream,
Expire, with the brilliance of untouched silver...
Cold rises from the linens of my young bed...
Nakedness chills me, white nakedness, chaste nakedness...

God of sex, who did not designate my body for Acceptance,
Who commended my ardent flesh to solitude,
Have mercy on my sighs of longing!

Grant me the embrace of hot and wild limbs!
Grant me red heat and flames, grant me the pleasure of
    pagan orgies!
Nakedness chills me, nakedness in vain, nakedness for
    no one!

1897

The Deflowering of the Soul

> *O! Unerbittlich*
> *In seiner Zukunft*
> *Ist das Gewesene!*
> Conrade, Trauer[1]

Life, that brutal pimp, led my soul out to the marketplace,
And revealed her beauty to lechers. Look, a harlot!
It sold my nakedness to satyrs' instincts and sent me to languish,
Stifled by the rude lust of seaside taverns...

In the hothouse of Vice and Fornication you blossomed, O flower of my soul!
In coital purple you were garbed early on, and scintillating gems of sin
Adorned your nakedness... Green myrtle was braided into your hair,
And you were made to keep time with your foot to the sound of the Berecynthian flute...

---

1 Oh! The past / is pitiless / in its future!

O Pleasure! I have crawled through all of your lairs,
Inhaled all of your perverse aromas,
And long breathed the stench of your harvest of rancid
    fruit!

Wearied by the ennui of yesterday and wearied by the
    ennui of tomorrow,
I apathetically watch the loathsome rats of thought
Scurry through the sewers of my life so repulsively...
    so repulsively...

1897

Bacchanalia

I will create a new world for my soul,
And light a new sun over its cities.

It will be a world of naïve and primary colors,
It will be tones full of contrasts, without nuances.

It will be new pleasures and new impressions
And the most profound sensations and primordial
    feelings.

It will be air full of dancing gold
And full of flames and blazing like a furnace.

It will be the fulminating and chaotic boulevards of
    metropolises,
Babels, Romes and Sodoms, mutually interpenetrating.

It will be virgin forests overgrown with violent vegetation,
It will be gale-winds, roaring through the flattened
    grass of the prairies.

It will be a world that will bear rugged men,
Swarthy gymnasts with muscular, gigantic limbs.

It will be a world of love as attractive as a magnet
And strong as battle and hot as the fire of the heavens.

It will be the embrace of bodies squeezing each other
    like pythons intertwined,
The pleasure of their limbs crackling like fires through
    entire suburbs.

It will be the passion of crowds flowing through the
    streets on festival days,
In sharp and blending colors, in the din of barbarian
    music.

In the pounding of Flemish drums and kettledrums
    and the clatter of castanets,
In the jangle of hammered dulcimers, in the thunder
    of tambourines, in the clang of cymbals and zithers!

I want life! Intoxication! Sun and passion and wind!
The seething of blood! And change, without cease,
    eternally,

Flaming eyes and burning foreheads and blazing faces,
Fluttering hair and upraised arms and tramping feet,

I want rugged, brutal and athletic companions,
Swarthy athletes with muscular, gigantic limbs.

I want love that's elemental and fierce like a cougar's leap,
I want beating hearts like passionate bells to attract my soul.

I want companions who will come like barbarians in rows, in close ranks,
Faces, bodies, shoulders, upraised arms merged in unity,

That I might go with them, O Pleasure, ON A LONG JOURNEY,
In the agitation of a united mass, in solid formation,

That I might mix my youth with their strength, my passion with their passion,
And, in the hour of death, my blood with their blood.

1897

The Coming of the Barbarians

O n'y vouloir, ô n'y pouvoir mourir un peu!
Ah! tout est bu, tout est mangé! Plus rien à dire.[1]
                                              Verlaine

Everything is languid and oppressive, as though
    weighted down by sleep.
Day after whitewashed day, in the empty streets.
And night! Those long silences, as friends fall asleep
Amidst tedious carousing! (The ennui of it all!)

Last sons of an exhausted race,
Beneath a waning sun, on a soil bled dry,
We miserably subsist in our gilded rooms,
Waiting for red-haired barbarians to flood the City gates.

Do you not hear their calls? Those are the shouts of
    men from Geba!
Calling for white flesh, with furious lust they pound
    on the doors!

---

1 O not to want, not to be able, just a bit, to die! / Ah, all is drunk, all is eaten! Nothing more to say!

(We have known everything for so long now! Ah,
   everything reeks of the plague!)

No longer to want anything! How boring you are,
   Kritobul, in your love!
Your naked lips tremble as though scorched with blood!
(Ah, another *light*! To see everything anew!)

                                              1897

My Poetry to the Reader

My beautiful love, as once pale Selene
Descended in a dream into the body of a shepherd,
So I too will come down into you. Into your heart I
    will sink,
To make it tremble, yearning, with atoms of silver,
    forever.

My rhythm, my music will resound in you henceforth,
As into an abyss, your fate will melt into me,
I know an alchemy of words that can transmute
Reality into the glitter of gold, the flame of Eternity.

May the smile of my beauty, future love,
Heal your sick body, as from my dreams it gushed:
Not poems, I have given you a DREAM, which is
    greater than life.

And when the kiss of my lips enthralls you forevermore,
Wounded by my beauty, you always will adore
What I now adore: solitude, vanity, night.

                              1905

The Emerald Plaque

My soul, burn with your own longing in solitude,
And not only from people—into the distance flee
From their thoughts. As the sea creates
Coral in its depths, burn inside with your own dreams.

You are more triumphant than feeble Orpheus.
You escape the maenads, the lowest lust,
That they may not drag you, like others, into their filth.
Charmed by your own music, you stare, longing, into
    dusk.

May inert matter be animated by your dreams,
Enlivened by the sense of eternity and the breath of fate.
Like a work of marble, sculpt all of your days.

May the solitude of your dreams not be lifeless:
May thought, like a magic bee, always resound in it
In its own restive and vigorous rhythm.

                                      1905

Sin

Pour fire into my gloom, you who refract, as a prism
Into colors, my life into the miracle of sins.
As on a drum grown mute in silence, within my soul,
 pound,
For the player of passion must beat to make the
 instrument resound.

As the icy breath of wind on the glass of a hothouse,
 so breathes
Doubt in the seclusion where the flower of days grieves.
O sin, in my life may your pride shine forth again,
In the purple flower of the tropics may my days flame
 up again.

As hot blood gushes out beneath the sword, may my
 Song
Now, beneath your blow, gush out,
And transform into ecstasy my distress and my doubt.

May it thunder through eternal darkness, may it pierce
 the bright stars,
May it cast a blasphemous glance into the abyss of
 Nothingness,

Then, disdaining everything, may it collapse, and be extinguished.

1905

Classical Triptych on Love and Song

Syrinx Sings:

Fleeing you, evil satyr, in the shade of delicate golds,
I sank into the river's depths. In silent dreams
So often had I gazed into its mirror.
Now, hunted, I was turned into a wavering reed.

And yet, cruel one! In horror I suddenly saw
My former life plunge like a stone into the depths.
To preserve the purity that slept in my body's snow,
I was destined now to be a mere thing forever.

Where are the joyful roses of my lips, where is the
    alabaster of my face?
Where are my eyes now, shadowed by long lashes?
Where is the heavy flow of my hair, in dark blue waves?

Of all things lost, may your love return at least one:
My voice! Break this reed, and put it to your lips!
I want at least to cry out my pain in song.

Pan Sings:

Not from my love did you flee, nymph: your eyes
Beheld my body, so repulsive to your hopes,
And were appalled. They forgot that though
Descended from the gods, I have legs but of a goat.

I loved you. As of a miracle I dreamed
Of sweet kisses as my lips were sucking grapes,
And I saw the fount of your eyes like flaming gold
In the grapes' skin, which the sun's brilliant glare penetrated.

I dreamed of the moment when, intoxicated by feminine embraces,
Tenderly, I would whisper words into her enchanted ear,
But now into an ordinary reed my longing only gazes.

Am I to turn my love into song? On the syrinx
Am I to merely play, while other gods kiss, and grasp the body?
Robbed of love, to others of love am I to sing?

The Poet Sings:

Just sing of the love that others live with passion.
Sing your melody, by others' pleasure inspired,
In this delusive world, where you are mute to yourself,
Then retreat within yourself, a reptile, by all despised.

Watch impassively as fate rends you while it exalts others.
Play your own pain to the hypocrite and liar.
Hide your abased dream in the depths of an icy soul,
And veil emotion with silence as a face with a heavy visor.

When the syrinx falls from your lips, weary unto death,
Perhaps then new dreams shall daze your heart with
    languor,
But cripple them with cold, and hold them in contempt.

Have the strength to shatter your feelings
Without fear, so they scintillate frigidly like icy gems,
And then watch impassively, as everything collapses
    into nothingness.

1905

Karel Hlaváček

Preface to the Collection
In the Wee Hours

It was in the wee hours... I walked, overly wearied by kisses, which had descended on me for the first time in my life like a heavy shower of spring rain. Beyond the river the pale radiance of faded gold heralded the imminent rise of the moon, and the entire indistinct landscape, devoid of outlines, adrift in the pallid and timorous light, seemed to have been waiting all night, since early evening, for its first rays. There was a peculiar, strained silence, disturbed only by the deep, drawn-out sounds of trumpets from a distant village band, which was apparently finishing its Sunday performance... The moon rose listlessly, reddish; it paled and began to tremble on the river; everything seemed to kneel in united prayer... And all of this somnolence, longing, exquisite languor and giddiness diffused an odd, delicate and rare mood into my soul. It was like something for the deepest tones of a French horn, for the deepest tremolos of glass flutes, for the melancholy solo of an inherited viola (and moreover, one that is muted by an ivory damper)... A tepid, balmy infusion, the bitter aroma of fennel oil, pressed into an antique carved from green Egyptian diorite by a femininely delicate, unknown aristocratic hand—a hand perfumed with the heady scent of crimson lacquer... I ground the most delicate nuances of colors, I guided my hand to the subtlest strokes, I experimented with the harmonies of the deepest minor chords and composed in the most dangerous keys and signatures, until I approached the realization of my visions. To capture everything sublime, mysterious, anemic and timorous in delicate mystifications, in irony and in warm intimacy—to stir up, in a few kindred souls, through the brief prayer of a mage, the rare and mysterious mood spellbound in the words: *in the wee hours*—that is my domain, my *raison d'être*.

1896

Pseudo-Japonaiserie

Of course, as a worshiper of all that is rarefied and exquisite, he was also a pietist of small japonaiseries. Although he was convinced that fragrant dusks by bamboo marshes, sweetened by the scent of sugarcane, and sunny afternoons in tea gardens would glimmer in no other soul with such faith and harmony as in the souls of female Japanese artists, sometimes he transgressed against this belief. To perceive and reproduce the most silent wafting of moods through the spider webs of their souls without tearing the harmony with their awkward fingers, to surrender to rapture over a few ink spots on gold lacquer and the delicacy of a few basic colors, which, refracted side by side, were capable of breathing out all of the longing of solitude, all of the minute sorrows and imperceptible laments of childishly opened eyes—yes—in all of this his longing confusedly sought expression.

He felt a sort of kinship with those anemic beings, so overly capable of loving silent nights with big, naïve moons and white roosters flying up, carefully impasted with silver lacquer in a few brushstrokes above tea branches on blackened backgrounds... They used their own strange colors, just a few of their own strange brushstrokes, each one of which could express all of the subtlety of their miniature dreams, could capture in the branches clouds all atremble from fragrances and the cries of magnificent birds swimming in nighttime waters—and yet at the same time they destabilized everything to the point of sharp caricatures, and he was different from them only insofar as he wished to use, in lieu of colors and lines, words—smelted in the hermetic furnace of his refined style.

1896

The Vampire

It was in some gloomy landscape
   with the golden stain of the moon somewhere
   above, behind the clouds,
   in a strange landscape, fearful, diffuse, without shadow,
      without light,
   where I had never walked before,
   when I caught sight of him...

He loomed low and silent above me
   in the pale colors of a delicate old lithograph.
   His weary face, fair and pale,
   with the lamp of his green eyes beneath thick brows,
   atropinized my fearful eyes forevermore...
   He soared silently on a pair of vampire wings,
   metallically black and velvety, spread out in an
      enormous span,
   shading the entire sky,
   and as he raised them stars showered down,
   unperturbed, like an incandescent swarm of wild,
      metallic bees
   frightened by a tempest out of a primeval aspen
      wood...

The last scion of once-powerful ducal lines
flew through the strange landscape,
returning from his passionate, involuntary lovers,
the warm milk of future mothers and the blood of
   their breasts
on his thin, clenched lips.

It was in some gloomy landscape,
   fearful, with the golden stain of the moon,
   where I had never crept before,
   when I caught sight of him—
   the last sovereign of a once-powerful line,
   before which burghers, magnates and kings trembled
      in fear,
   and their silent and sickly young daughters
   yearned for him secretly for months and days...
   They yearned for his visits on silent moonlit nights,
   when they waited for his wings to enshroud their hot
      beds,
   for his presence to permeate their white flesh,
   and for his sticky, rough tongue to make the ailing
   eyelids of their enraptured eyes twitch sweetly at
   the painful sensations in their breasts.

Demon of uncanny nights, nights with the golden
      stain of the moon,
   fearful, diffuse nights,
   nights without shadow, without light,
   with weak gleams of lascivious primal instincts on
      the horizon:

You proud and white barbarian, lover of everything
    sick, pale,
  you dispassionate and yet fearful, noble madman,
  living on the left-over vital forces of virginal juices
  infected with hereditary atrophy,
  you symbol of decadence!
  Is the lair to which you retreat from me
  somewhere, perhaps, in the black landscapes of my
    Dukedom?
  I do not know—
  but on lonely, odd nights it seems to me
  that my soul leaves my body
  and suddenly grows vampire wings,
  beneath which, as I raise them, stars shower down,
    unperturbed,
  and through a fearful, diffuse landscape without
    shadow, without light,
  with the golden stain of the moon above, somewhere
    behind the clouds,
  my soul silently takes flight.

...And only later, towards morning, does it return,
    stupefied
  by the mystical orgy—
  and awaken in the quotidian parasite
  that will miserably drag out another day in the
    profane noise of the street,
  as it did on the accursed day preceding,
  and will again on the repulsive day to come.

                            1896

She Has Come

Did you hear, my soul, her step lingering below,
    from the moats of our Castle, so carefully locked?
    Towards our shuttered windows she called, time and
        again: *Hallo!!...*

The night was so silent outside—and in the hallways
        of the Castle all was dead,
    only a heart beat so fearfully in prayer in the last
        chamber,
    like a family prisoner tapping on the walls,
    time and again, with a gaunt finger, timidly,
    in the paternal dungeons...

The moonlit night was so silent outside when the crisis
        was to set in,
    and for the first time *she* was to come, long
    Anticipated,
    Feared,
    late;
    only towards morning...
    And she has come.

With her inaudible, lingering step in our mournful
    Loneliness,
long abandoned by all of the living...

Did you hear, my soul, her lingering step below,
    from the moat of our Castle, so carefully locked?
    Towards our shuttered windows she called, time
        and again: *Hallo!!...*
    She had to come,
    if our ancient kingdom is to end with me,
    with me,
    heir of all the weaknesses of our impotent line
    (though my young life cannot be guilty of all of
        their Sacrileges
    and cannot be blamed for all of the debaucheries of
        the damned).
    I am but the last sickly scion, deprived of will,
    bound by fate,
    a feeble reflection in the dark of a proud pennant,
    faded long ago by a mournful sun,
    which once displayed the glory and renown
    of my ancestors
    to their subjects from the highest tower
    in purples, golds and blues...

All of them have gone now...
    Only at night are the silenced hallways and
        drawbridges haunted by
    their vows, which they never honored,
    their sins, which were ignored,
    their diffident looks, extinguished without
        gratification,

and curses, in which righteous indignation still
 trembles,
declaimed in the ecstasy of a hymn on the heads of
 the rebellious,
in the sumptuous ceremonials of ecclesiastical
 assemblies,
pronounced in Italian by a bishop serving in Latin...
Mothers of my effeminate virtues!
Fathers of my inherited sins!
Rest in peace:
quietly and without witnesses,
proud, without the sympathy of others,
with me the sad tragedy of our line will end—
and humiliating.

—suddenly everything is becoming clear,
 the strange white dawns
 that once awkwardly bathed the splendid gardens
  of your brains too
 are rising, growing slowly and majestically into a
  flood.
 Mysterious, white, impermeable mists
 fill my head, weakened by fear—
 images wander apprehensively, unchained now,
 arms stretched out in alarm,
 in the confused whisper of blind men fleeing,
 left by a helping hand at the critical moment
 in the middle of the road so it too might take flight
  in terror...
 And a shadow, large and somber, already creeps
 through the mist
 with that lingering, indifferent step,

as it had trod the paths of my ancestors...
Fathers of my sins!
Mothers of my virtues!

Do you hear her step lingering below?——
From the moats of the Castle time and again she calls
towards our shuttered windows: *Hallo!...
Friend! Open!! Hallo!!!*——

1896

I Have Tuned My Viola

I have tuned my viola as low as it will go,
and late in the evening I sing my quiet song.

An ardent player of moods gloomy and sad,
I want to have the quaint magic of old, ironic ballads.

And on my inherited viola I play only to those who
    listen,
to those who hearken on unsure nights, towards
    morning, to the distance...

My melodies want to have the sadness and the pain
of everything that has grown, blossomed and ripened
    for no one, in vain.

And to have the hope and vague tenderness of all
that wants to sprout in the dense soil of a distant shore,

and to evoke a sound, timid but refined, that
    intoxicates the senses,
like the trembling of strong wires muffled by dampers,

and they long for intimacy in the still of prolonged
    staccatos,
when they're about to weep in the lowest pitches
    through the darkness...

On my inherited viola I play only when, I play only
    when
the moon is just about to rise, and darkness still covers
    the land,

and beyond the forests and water austere vigils fall,
and through the land the great mystery of *Holy Feasts*
    walk,

My slender fingers on the strings always tremble with
    emotion
when, late in the evening, I sing my quiet song...

I have tuned my viola as low as it will go.

1896

Anemia

Sad laughter, so intimate on its lips, yet still laughter...
Impassive, the southern night slowly lingers,
and my idée fixe, complacent towards everything,
gains on it slowly, with the peculiar gait of the timid.

They walk through the dark vale of hereditary Anemia,
where the morose moon that rises towards morning is
    dull,
where for ages all has been pale and the air has grown
    thin,
and anyone gone anywhere has wearied once and for all.

In silence they walk, sometimes they anxiously cough,
cholerically, and stop in the diaphanous mist,
and each lifts a furtive hand to her brow,
to the Alps crouched above, immobile and still,

and again they walk... Alas, knowing that in the twilight
    around
nothing in exquisite giddiness has lived to ripen, to
    blossom,

and the father is to blame that even the sweetest *come to me*
could bring back nothing, and cannot, and will not.

1896

The Primeval Submarine Forests

The primeval submarine forests did not even quiver,
only drawn-out Breath wandered the impassable
    pathways,
from submerged cities bells tolled weakly through the
    water:
at the Promised Shore in the darkness everything gazed.

A midnight prayer in their soaked lips,
lilies knelt, their whiteness unstained,
and black dolphins, keeping watch on the hill-tops,
died by fires in wordless pain.

And only in the wee hours, emerging above the shores,
to the singing of multitudes, to the glory of banners,
from a dream I heard the kneeling of silver forests

in the distant waters of the sea, at the capes of Mystery...
And in gardens of weakly blushing coral,
dark shadows impatiently thronged and quivered...

1896

The Subtlety of Sorrow

Foreword

Before half-closed eyes, in a few strokes in the foreground, the gloomy evening landscape grayed in the distance, with a bit of green gold in the west and the gentle andante of the horizon's blue... A model of subtlety conjured in a dream. An airy hallucination tuned in three colors with a pious mood...

A small boat sadly floats in the immeasurable distance without oars in the green gold...

Small porcelain towers of an intimate formalism, founded by artists on nearby hilltops, wait for warm winds from sweltering shores at moments of inspiration, or at least light gusts... The white pennants start to flutter... Wind from the sea!... And tiny porcelain bells, set in sway by the wind, again ring out the motif of the Loreto litany in the mystical silence, and the boat without oars hastens to the jetties.

In the bottom of the boat sits a comely cretin (do not lament!) with a refined and delicate brain, pressing his head to the side of the boat in a rigid pose, half kneeling, half reclining, hopelessly watching the fading gold of the sunset. The warm wind of someone else's inspiration ruffles his flaming blond hair, and he ardently sings...

It is his attenuated soul that sings, slender and sickly, wandering somewhere up there on that blurred gold, already burned up to a reddish brown—and neither lips nor ears know of its song... It ceaselessly sings the same hopeless, supremely naïve ballad of a rare lucidity, in the two verses of which his trite poetic head, years ago, during his captivity, had sung out all of its delicate sorrow over the loss of its only Friend...

The Intellectual's Inclination Towards the Character of a Spider

Confused, the hallucination of slight, dimmed light fled into the barren, cold darkness, frightened by that silently tolling knell of reality... Forms slowly died out into the silence... He was gradually becoming aware...

It appeared to him as an enigmatically inexplicable (for his subtle brain no longer apprehended the import of death)...and nonetheless entirely definite and irreversible fact.

Here it lies in the darkness on his violet, translucent palm—a black stain with a white cross on its tiny, gaunt backside—and he above it, incapable of utterance or exclamation... He bathes its corpse—soft and still tepid in his fine and delicate palms, veiled in a spider web—in the apprehensively long gaze of his dilated pupils, opalescent as jasper in the gloom of the prison cell. A silent sorrow agitates the ashen complexion of his fair face.

Not a human sorrow—for the sounds of human speech had long ago evaporated from his throat—but the sorrow of a wretched individual, in whom the weighty and sumptuous verbal apparatus of a former intellectual has been filtered down to delicate spider sibilants, and whose brain has been leveled to the perfect comprehension of the delicate caprices of eight spider eyes and the benevolent gestures of several pairs of spider legs. Sorrow from another life, other causes, the sorrow of intimately observed landscapes, the overly rarified sublimate of minute moods, sorrow slipping away from human language, which vainly makes compromises in all known manners of expressing, of capturing on its roughly cut edges the silkily agitated sheen of sorrow's nuances...

And the moaning of unknown seas from down there, from some great depth, from darkness, now thinly and steadily tolls a long, but on the whole entirely indifferent knell for the death of the Spider.

An Essential Feature of His Way of Life

Even sweet *self-satisfaction*—though rare, given his bodily weakness, but nonetheless necessary under the circumstances of long years of imprisonment—which would engulf him from time to time in violet dizzy spells, had lost much of its former inquietude. It was now merely the full grasping of the self, the silent adoration of the self for want of another sensual divinity. It was an act of self-comprehension and chastity, a tepid muscatel infusion, after which the eyelids half close and five or six blissful spasms silently course through the body... He had lost all of the violence of his former human cruelty and ferocity—only his wide-open eyes oddly trembled and his limbs silently surrendered to that rare sacrifice. He was no longer that enraged bull that would storm into abandoned gardens full of pure lilies to taint their whiteness with his rank drool; he was now an orphaned infant, a vampiric character after his father, who had died of a venereal disease, and who had merged the silent cretinism of a sexual madman with some kind of delicate credo of a subtle scribbler.

The Emergence of His Fixed Idea

When he first caught sight of him in the prison cell, he had fled from him, but he soon befriended his soft look, his silent breath, his dear presence. He concluded a willing compromise with him the instant he saw the virtuosic weaving and strong fabric of his spider web.

The yearning for air (the image of which now only as the wide azure, vaguely agitated him) was precisely what, not so very long ago, had led to the practically slavish attachment of his soul, the soul of an intellectual, to the arachnid physiognomy, to the low soul afflicted with cretinism. With anxious interest he would watch the *Spider* at work for entire days, weeks, months, years; sometimes he would endeavor to shorten his labor for him with naïve ironies, entertaining anecdotes, Voltairean paradoxes, and even witty pantomimes, and at the same time he would gather the agonizingly meager result of his daily work and process it with his trained and patient fingers...

A thought had long ago forced itself obstinately into his refined brain, which had lost all power of deduction: *to weave from spider webs a rope so strong: that it would bear away his body, so long: that it would bear him down to freedom, down to that melancholy sea, which he could hear roaring indistinctly in the darkness...*

Whither? And hundreds of other questions. Those simply did not exist for him. The fixed idea of freedom had completely annulled their gravity and urgency in favor of its triumphant darkness. He nourished him, he cared for him...only so that that he could steal the necessary material from him. And the farther he went beyond the limits of the possibility of becoming a Spider in thought, emotion and desire, the more piously he clung to this bizarre friendship, and the more he felt the entire weight of his own egoism.

One of His Sensations of the Subtle

And now his only companion, voluntary sufferer and problematic savior, had died... He reposes with dim, yellowish eyes and convulsively broken legs here, on his violet, translucent palm.

From down there, from somewhere deep down, the moaning of unknown seas resounds in a delicate and long, but on the whole indifferent death knell...

And there, beyond that moaning, there, far away on the deserted shores beneath eternal twilight—there is elegance, intimacy, refinement... Just close your weary eyes, be silent and hear... The gracious chords of three extended tones of some kind of unknown wind instruments imitate the subtle march of a forgotten carol...

A weary camp of thoughts lines up again in long regiments... And now they silently set off, bent forward, in the measured tempo of shepherds and shepherdesses, for a land sloping up towards the unknown. They walk through misty landscapes, in the despair of six-month nights... Only the dim phantom of the magnetic dawn gleams in delicate red shawls above the forests, the distant forests, and the bays of primeval Silence. The slender steeples of faraway churches sadly emerge, inundated by periodic floods. Just now they are celebrating an anniversary there, and a host of beautiful Madonnas, who have stepped down from their gold-plate backgrounds, are spending the night at the palace chapel at a meeting, which, to be sure, is lasting much too long (they wish to welcome him with the miracle of their immaculate bodies, preserved from prying eyes for several centuries by the heavy, rich vesture of the Middle Ages, and, oddly, always with the monotonously stereotypical folds of the school of one particular master...)

The march's triad has suddenly fallen silent. Another flood has inundated the church... the meeting has abruptly ended—and from below, there from the depths, somewhere from the darkness, the unknown sea again relentlessly roars that knell of mourning and silent despair.

The Burial Song over the Corpse

So he was dead, now, just when he was starting to have faith in his promising hopes of fulfilling his fixed idea. And those awkward outbursts of his rampant egoism, obsessed with air and the wide, indistinct azure, would now also come to naught...

He mourned the Spider, who until now had been no more than a friend.

His infirm and diffuse muscles, opalescent with the almond shine of a surgical preparation composed of freshly extracted alcohol, were shaken by hallucinations of subtle sadness that ran through his arteries in rectilinear, converging impulses all the way to the end of his slender fingers and silently drummed on the pliant walls of his long nails, the nails of a practiced weaver.

An infinite sadness for something unexpressed that he saw continuously eluding him always ran through his nerves when he heard the sea roar weakly... A sadness that you cannot understand, a most rare and reticent sadness, the sadness of faraway mountain ranges that no one has ever crossed, the sadness of new lines, whose subtleties cannot be captured in the rough constructions of your words and in the crude and sullied mirror of your profane expression...

In his blessed, quiet alto, now he sang to him a magnificent and magical burial song in new rhythms, preserving at the same time the loyalty of extinct family lines, piously opening the sickly richness of his thin lips... In the same stiff pose, half kneeling, half reclining, on his long, violet, translucent fingers the silkily shiny and still tepid corpse with the white cross on the gaunt backside...

And from somewhere below, from the depths, the sea roared out to him a demonstrative and humbly hesitant, but nonetheless altogether indifferent death knell.

1896

Vengeful Cantilena

I

O my Manon! I am no more the shy abbé
Who would go to fair Manon, from ennui ill and faint,

And whose presence gave her hope: today he may
   grow bold
And begin the promised legend of the sin of yellow
   roses...

O my Manon! Get used to it! Today my voice is too loud,
And, like the Gueux, of hunger alone may I be proud.

Defiantly I've left my companions and my home
So as to sing to you a cantilena to viola,

A vengeful cantilena, in which my lips, feebly,
Would reproach you for being weak more from hunger
   than ennui,

And my eyes, devoid of warmth, would grow strong
From this legend, as the moon goes blind from
   weeping long.

I know that all of this will unsettle my Manon,
Who would rather feign the customary longing for
    someone,

But meanwhile everywhere an awkward and drowsy
    silence
Descends upon the gardens, welcoming *someone else*.

II

Our barren lands are dark—not even the sick moon
    glows,
They emit no scent, no warmth, and vainly do we sow—
But softly, softly, Gueux, it seems it must be so.

The bells are languid, impotent—they do not rouse at all,
You may ring no alarm, and it's hours till the dawn,
But softly, softly, Gueux, you must retain your calm.

And line up on the long plains, and with blades in
your vengeful fists
Set out into the darkness and march on the sleeping
    Cities—
But softly, softly, Gueux, behind the plaintive winds.

And on the road lost in the fields steal up before the
    gates,
Cast lots to see who first his angry fist shall raise—
But softly, softly, Gueux, you must avenge our race!

III

It was a guileful kyrie that moaned at dusk through
    the empty plains,
For our fields, grown barren from long fear—
It was a prayer for warmth that our voices, exhausted
    and faint,
Entreated for our wives, grown barren from long fear.

It was a guileful kyrie for our bald young wives;
Slinking through the dark, we prayed for them and
    sighed,
With each famine without complaint we died for
    them in our lives—
But by *this* famine, Lord, by *this* famine we did not
    want to die!

And when again, in passionate embrace,
Our last wives were dying, grown barren from long fear,
With clenched, vengeful fists and clenched, vengeful
    glances,
We vilified your name and shouted wildly to the fields:

That *this* passion—you hear?—you hear?—we never
    shall subdue
In our swarthy bodies, nor sacrifice to you!

IV

Beneath a sad sky, a low sky, a sky devoid of warmth,
Someone walked along the river. It was a drowsy day.

Another drowsy day. Someone in the distance wistfully
    sang:
That all is vain, that nothing will grow, that nothing
    will take flame.

And everyone had fearfully gone to bed, turned out
    the lights—
The night was dank, the mood was cold—
When suddenly they recalled that it's no use to think
    of the fields,
That this year too nothing would come up of what
    they'd planted years ago.

The moon was in the clouds, in the sad clouds, a
    moon devoid of warmth,
The night was silent, someone walked along the plains
On the riverbank, singing a wistful song:
That all is vain. That nothing will grow. That nothing
    will take flame.

V

Around haggard faces tangled hair waved
(The whole day was foggy, and evening too was foggy
    and sorrowful),
And though they could surely have been at the tower
    by eight,
And the evening was unusually dreary and dismal,
They waited even so, with deceitful smiles, in the fog.

Taming wild hair on stooped necks,
Spiteful smiles (yet deceitful) on thin faces,

Their gaunt fists beneath their cloaks surely clenched,
They had stood since noon, head to head, in the arcades...

Then slowly the clock struck... The hour of judgment and salvation...
He was dragged in a cage, through the dark, in the fog.
O wild, bass voices! O vengeful faces!
Now they roar out in chorus—a derisive chorus (yet deceitful),
For if everything lied, their derision was most lying of all!

The evening was desolate, unusually dreary, and dismal.

VI

My naïve white barbarians! I am writing this to you—I, a redhead! Look closely on your sorrowful pilgrimage for two eyes, two pallid and reticent eyes. Many of you have passed by them indifferently, and you were always insensitive and impassive towards those two hapless eyes. Yesterday I stopped in front of them in a long, silent prayer—and when I recalled you as well, they complained wordlessly for a long time. So look for them in your dreams, look for them in ancient prayers, look for them in the songs of wistful and forgotten poets... That is where you are most likely to find them. Their whites have turned a sickly yellow and the silver of their gaze has blackened with time. They hold thousands of bowed oars, lances and bugles... Tremble before them, for there is horror in them, my white barbarians! But never be indifferent to gazes you meet by the roadside, lamenting.

You may meet them while sailing with them on the walls of a family cabin on sailboat passed down from father to son to grandson. There you see angular heads like Great Danes' with the infinite tenderness of small grayish eyes, ironic eyes, like only the Flemish have... Have respect for them, for those eyes have grown pallid with a strange yellow tinge, and they are fearful from the constant murmur of waves breaking against the side of the boat... Or go out among the smallest and watch children playing in the meadow. Pay special attention to those who are not joyful with the others and do not gather ragged robin, or anemone, or flaming poppies, but wander silently through the high grass by the swamp, stopping as though confused before the hemlock. (For a long time afterwards their small eyes give off the bitter and deadly scent...) And on dank and rainy afternoons, when everything smells like moist sand and the shore is deserted and the sea indifferently tosses waves, go out onto the sandbanks. In the green waves big, beautiful eyes shine with the familiar gleam of a milky pearl cast up by a wave. And nothing is greater than their sadness, nothing is greater than their silence. (Do you remember the beautiful legend of the dolphin that I told you once on the lake? And do you remember the cursed poet whose whole life was one bright hymn to the glory of the Sea?) The tenderness of the song is vanishing in the wind, its golden hues are paling—and nothing is sadder than the sadness of those two eyes, the eyes of a cursed poet.

But if you should have enough courage and strength, my white barbarians, on bleak and dismal nights stay up and pray behind closed doors. And only when the light in your lantern begins to pale and your hearts start to tremble with fear and your hands weaken with terror while praying—cast a quick glance at your treacherous and profound eyes that know how to lie more than a dream, more than an ancient prayer or the song of a forgotten poet—and tremble. There in the depths you will meet the eyes, a stranger's two eyes, eyes that are ironic and treacherous, grown fearful from the constant murmur of the waves breaking against the side of the boat—and you will meet a stranger's overly bitter gaze, the gaze of two eyes that grew up too soon and that have not been promised a long life, for they emit the bitter and deadly scent of hemlock. And way down at the bottom, there in the depths where everything has the pervasive scent of moist sand and where the sea indifferently tosses red shells in green waves, two eyes will gaze upon you, the eyes of a poet whose life was one solemn cry in praise of the Sea and whose song is now vanishing in the wind, its golden hues paling. Oh, have pity on the mist of all of those eyes!

And do not grow wise! Look only inside yourself, inside yourself, if dreams, ancient prayers and poets lie to you too little.

VII

Hairy fingers have slept on the organs since evening,
    utterly drained,
And someone has masked tears for ages beneath a red
    mane,
For everything lied here—even the candles, dying out
    in the dark,

Even the pictures of saints—oh, those pale faces may
   have lied most of all.

Everything lied here, everything. Even the musk's scent
   was feigned,
Even the moon, weary from vain efforts to wake,
Even the large, hairy hand, fearfully sleeping by dawn,
And the red mane—oh, the red mane may have lied
   most of all.

The moon sank with fatigue, exhausted in vain...

And irascible hands that fought wildly by habit each day
Woke up from the shadows, where they'd slept in a
   languishing faint,
The long, thin fingers that lied most of all
So fearfully approached, from silence, the upper octaves,
And played a hushed impromptu—a fearful
   impromptu they played.

VIII

It's evening, and the black clouds drift
Through a land that is barren and sick,
And to the Lord's Angel they pray...
In silence they kneel on the plain,
With a mood of irony
On them wearily smiling.

It's the sinful evening of a weary day,
With them no one prays.

And the black clouds to the Tower drift
That slumbers by the water in the mist,
They rest their arms on it...
But the weary bells are impotent,
By illness drained they drowse,
Never to be roused.

It's the sinful evening of a weary day,
Not even my bells will pray.

And the pious clouds go on their way
With their prayers in vain,
And with their silent rue...
And my russet mood
Wearily smiles on the mead
And says to them ironically:

It's the sinful evening of a weary day,
In our land no one prays.

IX

It was a rainy dusk, and across the river the wind was afraid,
And the lights were afraid, and the sick dogs were afraid
That fearfully barked now and then from the waterlogged cliffs,
Oh, since last night they had feared, they feared the desolate villages.

Though last night they'd been driven with shouts from
    their homes,
And they'd fled cross the river, where the wind fearfully
    moaned,
The sick dogs still barked, barked from their
    waterlogged chests,
And their weary voices trembled at times from the cold.

In the huts, by lamplight, they'd been testing the
    weapons they'd honed,
And towards midnight a herald had rushed through
    the village alone,
Shouting the signal: Let it be! Off to the plain!
Then, cursing, they drove all the dogs to the cliffs, far
    away,
And they themselves rioted, alone on the waterlogged
    plain.

X

A hundred or so sat in the square at empty tables
(It was a festive evening, and their god flashed
    brimstone in the sky for this festive day),
And they furtively squinted from up high down at the
    city hall...
Oh, in the city they'd captured the bishop, for his
    vehement faith.

Oh, they'd caught the fat bishop who'd claimed to eat
    his god
And sent landknechts against them, and scornfully put
    down their faith,

They'd prepared a feast from the bishop, the most
esteemed bishop,
And their god flashed stifling brimstone in the sky for
this festive day.

So stiffly the hungry sat in the square on this festive day,
And greedily they squinted towards the city hall, over
their empty plates.

XI

He'd patched up his gnawed leather apron already a
week past...
And today he waited for the sleepy moon to set and
sleep to settle on the land—
When it had set and the landknechts slept, he saddled
his gaunt, repulsive nag
And silently rode through the castle settlement,
crooning his "La la lan."

He trotted through the fields until they doused the
lights and fell asleep from waiting,
And when it was dark and silent, his features brightening,
he approached the arcade,
Hitched his nag up with a fox tail, his sweaty, ugly nag,
And, "I buy rats! I buy rats!" he sang out through the
hallways.

And at midnight, having bought them all, he drew his
gnawed apron tight
And through the fearful land, through the dreary land,
through the oppressive land

He rode on his gaunt nag, on his sweaty nag, on his
  ugly nag,
Soothing her in his hoarse tenor, beneath red whiskers,
  "La la lan."

XII

All is dead now, all is dead, the land doesn't even sigh,
All is vain, all is vain, revolt and defiance are over now,
And in the deadly silence vengeful shouts will never
  again resound.

Vain prayers rot in the fields on the festering bodies
Of those who bore the mark of the Gueux on their
  sunken cheeks
And who avenged it on the Croesuses, with their
  endless feasts.

Over the corpses on the field sulfurous flames still glow—
O my vain Manon, this is death, this is the end,
My viola's strings feel it too—Manon, cry with them,
For the kingdom of the Gueux is dead—oh, it had to
  be so.

1898

Otokar Březina

Art

O melancholy cemetery, where the souls of the Great
    dream,
and a congregation of resplendent shades enters the
    graves
of the centuries, the glow of mystical fires, like the
    polar shine,
casts its reflection on your gates!

Hypnotized by your luminosity, I approach your garden,
where a field of dead flowers in deep blue attire gleams,
glowing like azure phosphorus, as the night floods in,
like a bay of black seas.

Respiring mute words, time has stretched out mists of
    extinguished passions
on the grief of your silence, like gray yarn;
the heavy sigh of dead multitudes rises towards you
    from the fields,
and in your atmosphere rots.

O Eternal One, tell me if I may, unclean by the longing
    of my blood,

where Your cathedral of metal towers over the city of
    marble,
read my silent mass to You by the small altar
beneath the side vault?

On the altar table that shelters the ordained
into the wine of life's ecstasy may I dip my bread
beneath the roses of my dreams and the lights of the
    prayers
of the relics of Your dead?

Will the grapes of Your body yield their miraculous blood
in the gold of the chalice, in my weak hands a weight,
will You illuminate my vision, born only for dusk,
with the light of angels?

On the frontiers of my days I pray that You torment
    and burn me,
and in prisons of anguish whiten my face to snow,
and in an incense of thanks I will burn my grief into
    fragrances
for You in the fire and rhythm of poetry!

As white blossoms on purple rugs I will spread before You
the foam of pleasure, cast up by love's seething,
and the bliss of maidenly bodies, where, cast in the
    form of breasts,
fragrance in alabaster sleeps.

My soul will radiate up to the heavens, an incandescent
    column,

and in the coffin of my strength, as in pewter, I will lie
 down to sleep,
when I collapse at Your altars in the convulsions of
 Mystery,
like a defeated priest.

1895

The Gaze of Death

Oftentimes, I know, at bedsides and in twilights of premonition,
before your triumphant gaze my gaze has been extinguished.

In mine weakness and longing, in yours the glistening laughter of steel,
and I glimpsed my own thought within its mirror.

She walked pale and confused into the distance of unknown Cities buried in snow,
into gloom and polar nights along the mute weariness of roads.

The anguish of doubt had frozen in her face, and the cold of timeless space
Had bound her feeble, tortured limbs in metal raiment.

In the folds of vanishing forms, as from the flower of a mystical tree,
through the mists, from your eyes snow was shaken down in heaps,

and it thickened and darkened, absorbed radiance,
    whisked it up, and blew it about,
and as though on pale crimson flames melted on the
    wounds of my thought.

Oftentimes, I know, at bedsides and in twilights of
    premonition,
before your fixed gaze my gaze has been extinguished.

Pale, spellbound, mute, like a sleepwalker lured from
    his bed,
hypnotized by the Unknown, with my dream I tread,

and, lit by your eyes, the lights of funeral torches,
clutched in the feeble hands of my days, tremble
    faintly before me.

1895

Apostrophe to Autumn

Bright October days, in which the pure azure gleams
   and from bronze boughs blaze crimson leaves,
   which, wafted down by a gust of autumnal breath,
   glitter as though of hammered gold!
In your cold aroma I scent, thawing, radiating heat,
the breath of deceased mornings and long-dead moods,
the sheen of yellow noons, when the sun's fervid breath
beats down on ripe fruits' sweetening pulp,
and the souls of fragrant evenings, burnt up
in the purple fires of sunset. From you a stifled
flock of departed birds wails, rejoices, sings to me
in an orchestra of tones. In you mingle and merge
the dream of wilted blossoms, the swish of cut grain,
the shimmer of extinguished colors, faded nuances
   and lights,
the flight of dead butterflies and the seething whirl
of myriad extinguished lives in the golden baths of day!
You are the feeble, dying pulse of mysterious forces,
when in peace and in sleep and in rest they unite!

Bright autumn days, in which the pure azure gleams
   and from bronze boughs blaze crimson leaves,

which, wafted down by a gust of autumnal breath,
glitter as though of hammered gold!
Spread your brilliance, blaze in cold October
with your luster of carmines, vermilions and siennas,
and pour out death, which trickles like a stream of rain
from your glimmering rays, as from a goblet wrought
of cold metal! Your heavy fragrance
like a noxious gas abides in the depths of my soul,
and the immense agony of colors, blossoms, life
like a bitter infusion I quaff from your air!

1895

Evening Prayer

Pour your mysterious sap into my ardent blood,
O death of living bodies, by which night turns into day,
Bind me in my bed with your mortal languor,
Like maidens' white arms, so soft is your embrace.
In your miraculous fragrance I scent another world,
Melt my earthly life, stir the heavenly into waves,
Placate in my soul my prayers' fervor and blaze,
Which burn upon my lips and flame red upon my face!

Incline, O sainted one, the dark lantern in my eyes,
Pour new oil into it, give my perception light,
That I may see thousands of miles with the ray of my
    gaze
Into the gloom of the sea's jungles and the glow of
    mountain heights;
How crystal presses to crystal in the cliffs' deepest womb,
How the radiance of colors in a web of blossoms
    descends,
How life awakens from slumber in matter's hidden
    depths,
In being's infinite flowering and eddy and ferment.

And heighten my mortal hearing, grant it increased
    strength,
Into an instrument of resonance reshape it,
That, like mysterious music, I may hear the rumble of
    growth,
And overspilling juices' undulation;
Let me hear the music of stellar paths and the plants'
    obscure pulse,
The refraction of rays of light, and the beat and hum
    of air,
Butterflies' silent flight, and in the depths of the soul,
The mysterious birth and struggle, whirl and dampening
    of thoughts.

Free my thought from earthly weight,
That at the speed of light in flight it may soar
Over the green sea and the realm of crystal and rock,
Into the pits of extinct volcanoes and the earth's
    molten core;
Let me fly like lightning through the night's eternal abyss,
Where seething streams gush from fiery springs
Into weeping caves, whose tears through the ages
Congeal into stony sleep beneath their baldakins.

And into the poles' long nights, where eternal ice and
    snow
In frigid brilliance scintillate on crystal cliffs,
To the bright land of the south, where the laughter of
    odalisques,
Like music in sultans' gardens, flutters and billows and
    ripples,
Above the din of nations and deserts' wordless sorrow,

Where, above black primeval forests and the sheen of
    alpine peaks,
The pulse and beat of life, in weakened rhythm, dies,
Above the pensive steppe and the prairies' green.

Let me grasp everything, the aims of all paths and roads,
All that I see live and grow, blossom, mature and die,
The eternal cycle of living forces, which clothes the
    constellations
In its gossamer nets, and which governs all fall and flight,
Which suffers in our souls, and gives the lily scent,
And in a bluish flame above the marshland gleams.
I am thirsty; let me drain, and become inebriated with
The wine of mystery, on the shores of eternity.

Permeate my body, and from your mysterious springs
Diffuse nepenthe through every muscle and nerve,
In the unknown rapture of your delirious fire
Spurt out like lava, and flame and flow and burn,
Until desire's incandescent breath, like a pitch torch,
    burns
Down to ashes in your mysterious blaze,
Then breathe onto my forehead and let me go to sleep,
An eternal, final sleep, from which I never shall awake.

                                      1895

Mood

Heavy, languid from the heat, on the trees a murmur falls
And hangs motionless, while in longing intervals
The oppressed forest breathes and a hot stream of sweat
And a coarse scent from fissured leaves mingles with
    its breath.
Beneath the rigid trees pale lethargy creeps,
Breathes foreboding in my face, settles next to me and
    speaks
With my melancholy soul in a language of dead words,
And within me the yearning for timeless mysteries stirs.
The sun's overripe blossom withers in white gleams,
Quivers in sprays of twilight and sinks through the
    blue leaves
Into the mute exhaustion of apathetic hush, and
    quenched
In moss, in springs of mysterious breath,
It lulls me with lassitude, as would slow waves
Of blood, flowing over me from my freshly opened veins.

                                                        1896

Dead Youth

On an old piano, in its sleeping metal strings,
As from quivering harps I heard a rhythm flow
That clung to the subtly vibrating wires
In a tearful dew of languorous, plaintive tones.

In my soul a thought arose like a heady scent,
And the song that in my youth I used to hear
Respired in my face and took me by the hand,
And led me through the silenced gardens of past years.

The heavens' beauty shimmered in brilliant constellations,
Dripping the magic of stars into time's silent streams,
Where in a glass coffin, like a sainted woman, dead,
My youth lay in a shroud of extinguished springs.

The bloom of rosy dreams blossomed in its cheeks,
And my tears' hard gems in a luminous diadem gleamed,
Mingling with the radiance of its fresh, young limbs,
Embalmed with the fragrant treasure of my pure
    memories.

And the warmth of dead charms, which, fresh,
    beckoned me,
Beneath the rosy veil that my days' dawn had woven,
The blaze of long looks that lie extinguished in my soul,
And dead kisses, whose fiery ardor left me cold;

The fire of embraces rendered cold by thought,
And the bitter blood of grapes, from which I sucked
    no bliss,
The rain of blossoms, wafted down, which once fell in
    my lap,
But died, at my hands' touch withered,

Dewy rainbows' languid flame, which bathed me not
    in cool,
The blaze of breaking dawns, which did not light up
    my face,
The faded light of white days, which turned my time
    into nights,
Like the luminous peace of night into turbid, graceless
    day,

All of this flared up in my soul, and in the music of
    dead hopes,
In echo trembled with anguished moaning, as I, in
    pensive mood,
Grieving, stood over the corpse of my own youth,
Like a lover over the dead girl he had seduced.

                                             1895

Anniversary

The familiar path I walked had changed in my eyes.
Trees loomed before me from the faded snow
Somehow differently from before. In shimmering green
The sunset faintly glowed, the burnt-out boundary of
   a dead day, strangely sad.

The horizon constricted in a tightening circle of steel.
Darkness ripened.
A black brotherhood of trees, I saw, knelt down to the
   earth
As to a choir praying for the dead. The sky's pall sank
   lower
Above my head, as though oppressed and stretched
   down by twilight.

And silence rose in a haze from the distance, fell from
the heights and, horribly solemn,
Muffled my footsteps. My soul's voice quavered with
   whispers of deference.
(There was something languid in the air, as though the
   burning thirst
Of incandescent Candlemas had drunk in all its
   freshness.)

This is the time when, on other days, with melancholy
    delight I would inhale
The long expiring of colors and lights and listen to the
    music
Of approaching shadows. A mysterious sense would
    speak to me
From the close proximity of night, the breath of eternal
    dreaming.

Today anguish blew on my face. And long-faded years
Rose up in my soul. My own breath seemed someone
    else's,
As though someone invisible were striding beside me,
Holding my trembling hand in a familiar clasp.

Oh, yes, Sainted Woman! Your festivity today in
    eternal gardens!
My thoughts sing a requiem, like an undulating chorus
In the warm lament of candles, where scarlet blood
    overflows the chalice
Of eternal light onto your altar, veiled in black.

The cool breeze of death fans the lace of shadows on
    the window of my soul.
A prayer of contemplative solitude compassionately
    presses my hand:
For the black veils of my memories, falling in folds,
Are a soft bed, marked forevermore with the impression
Of your dead body.

                                          1895

Scents of the Gardens of My Soul...

Scents of the gardens of my soul,
spilt down my weary cheeks in warm waves of languor,
scents raised from flowerbeds covered by a thousand
    nights!

You thicken into the quickened exhalations of
    swinging censers
(ghastly cactuses of smoke grown from a glowing grain)
amidst the muffled clinking of silver chains
during a pontifical funeral mass.

The fermented breath of peat-bogs and rotting mosses
over compressed layers of ash deposited by centuries,
scents of former moods, felled forests and extinguished
    springs!
Baths of poisoned mists over stagnant waters
in a landscape of dying vegetation
and in the deathly thirst of white summer torridity
that has drunk up all the silver dew from the calyces,
    faded from the heat,
and has drained the transparent moisture of the
    diffused shadows!

You are the scents of closed rooms
where, on a damp bed,
in the lassitude of medicinal essences and the gloom of
    lowered curtains
(as life sings beneath the windows in the last peals of bells
    and the ecstasy of sunshine),
my wakeful memory buries its head
in soft pillows of dreaming.

I sense from you the lament of dried sprigs of jasmine,
laid in a prayer book
by a trembling white hand.
The scent of rotten letters, where convulsive prayers of
    passion
that once kindled fire in long extinguished eyes
smoke from the faded script.

The scent of rooms in my father's house sold to a
    foreigner,
and the reproach that breathes from the folds of my
mother's rotting dress,
as she prays for me among the Saints.

The scent of burning candles on nights of lamentation
bound in violet chains of lightning,
and the scent smoldering from the black wick of a
    burnt-out candle
carried around the face of a dying man.

The smile of wilted violets
that no loving hand has picked for me

or given to me on my birthday.
The scent of mysterious flowers that wells up in rhythm
with the moaning of fountains
in the blue seclusion of locked parks (O lovers!),
to which no one has given me the keys.
The scent of flowing hair and the white trembling of a
    body
from which the rapture of nights raining stars poured
    into others' days,
while I saw no twilight at all.

Scents of the gardens of my soul,
scents risen from flowerbeds covered by a thousand
    nights!

Scents of palm groves and steppes blossoming with lilies,
potions sweetening as sunsets burn out,
comforting gusts of a cooler breath on my perspiring
    brow
from the shores of silent rivers that flow into the bays
    of Death!
O greetings borne on the wind from faraway oases,
O thundering hymn of invisible waterfalls
beyond the pale-blue mountain range of the promised
    land!
O scents of inaccessible islands beyond the dispersed
    mists of light, color, and form!
Beneath your clouds congregations of my dead dreams
staggered along, like processions of exhausted pilgrims
    to miraculous springs,
over hallowed hills and on to the cathedrals!

You have breathed on me with the life of those strange
   flowers,
which, closed to the sun, open themselves to the
   glorious silence of the stars:
at times of agonizing cold over the unexpressed cries of
   song!
over the mown and yellowed crop of longing past its
   bloom!
from the mystical wreathes of prayer by beds made for
   the last time!
in green dusks of languor that embraced me in the
   cathedral!
in the weary lowering of arms spread wide towards the
   serene shadow!
when a hostile soul approached me from belovèd eyes!
when I have waited in vain for the gold of dawn to
   blossom in polar nights
and for the cooling of the melancholy resonances,
from which stream forth, in low clouds of smoke,
the grief of the Past and the anguish of the Unknown.

                                           1895

Regret

I bear within my soul the regret of one confined to bed,
when the triumphant ringing of bells ripples down
   from the highest tower
(he has built altars to the Lord's Body with lilies
and let the sickly translucence of flames in silver
   candlesticks blossom in the fires of the sun),
when the steps of crowds are smothered in green carpets
   of flowers
and quake in broken rhythms from fragrant reeds with
   the warm exhalations of the waters,
when the greetings of gardens shine from the wreathes
   of maidens of honor,
and when thanks for life solemnly float with billowing
   sails over waves of smoke in a hymn to the Mystery
   of the Supreme Being.

I bear within my soul the regret of an impoverished
   ruler of boundless realms,
when, weary of life, he hears the corn splitting on the
   sloping edges of the cornfields:
clusters of silver needles scattered by the wind,

glistening swarms of bizarre insects settled on the
   sonorous stalks,
evenings fatigued by fragrances, reposing in the vineyards;
he hears his death knell in the ringing of scythes,
   his funeral song in cries of strength;
whose will be the crop of grain, where the rays of day
   have hardened into the shiny scales of serpents
and the blood of the earth into blackish grapes?

Who has breathed frost onto my windows and obscured
   the pure singing of colors?

In the white halls above my room evening chandeliers
   start to glitter,
with a smile mirrors return the cheerful blush to cheeks,
the cold glass starts to glow with the snow of perspiring
   breasts,
the air thickens with cries of laughter and fragrances.
The rhythmic beats of the dance!

I bear within my soul the regret of a prisoner on the day
   of May celebrations,
the regret of a lover at the door of the church on his
   wedding day,
the regret of one banished to the roar of artillery, who
   welcomes ships bearing flags of angry distant lands,
the regret of one exhausted from searching for dreams
   in the first blue light of dawn,
the regret of gazes worn out from vain waiting before
   departure,
the regret of fading faces that never blushed from kisses,

the regret of a foreigner touched by the naive embrace
   of a Christmas carol,
the regret of a musical instrument hung over the bed of
   a deceased maestro,
the regret of flowers that no one picked and no one
   sacrificed in vases on an altar,
the regret of light that burned out in a solitary lamp
and that no one put into the bedroom of lovers.

The hours of my past have left me, and I did not gather
   flowers for them,
the days came secretly, and I did not decorate them
   with roses, and I did not harvest their ripening rays,
the time of twilight has come, the wind of the Unknown
   is rising in the lanes,
and not one joyous song reaches me from afar.

                                                    1895

A PARTIAL LIST OF SNUGGLY BOOKS

G. ALBERT AURIER *Elsewhere and Other Stories*
CHARLES BARBARA *My Lunatic Asylum*
S. HEZOLNRY BERTHOUD *Misanthropic Tales*
LÉON BLOY *The Tarantulas' Parlor and Other Unkind Tales*
ÉLÉMIR BOURGES *The Twilight of the Gods*
CYRIEL BUYSSE *The Aunts*
JAMES CHAMPAGNE *Harlem Smoke*
FÉLICIEN CHAMPSAUR *The Latin Orgy*
BRENDAN CONNELL *Metrophilias*
BRENDAN CONNELL *Spells*
BRENDAN CONNELL (editor)
 The World in Violet: An Anthology of EnglishDecadent Poetry
RAFAELA CONTRERAS *The Turquoise Ring and Other Stories*
DANIEL CORRICK (editor)
 Ghosts and Robbers: An Anthology of German Gothic Fiction
ADOLFO COUVE *When I Think of My Missing Head*
QUENTIN S. CRISP *Aiaigasa*
LUCIE DELARUE-MARDRUS *The Last Siren and Other Stories*
LADY DILKE *The Outcast Spirit and Other Stories*
CATHERINE DOUSTEYSSIER-KHOZE *The Beauty of the Death Cap*
ÉDOUARD DUJARDIN *Hauntings*
BERIT ELLINGSEN *Now We Can See the Moon*
ERCKMANN-CHATRIAN *A Malediction*
ALPHONSE ESQUIROS *The Enchanted Castle*
ENRIQUE GÓMEZ CARRILLO *Sentimental Stories*
DELPHI FABRICE *Flowers of Ether*
DELPHI FABRICE *The Red Sorcerer*
DELPHI FABRICE *The Red Spider*
BENJAMIN GASTINEAU *The Reign of Satan*
EDMOND AND JULES DE GONCOURT *Manette Salomon*
REMY DE GOURMONT *From a Faraway Land*
REMY DE GOURMONT *Morose Vignettes*
GUIDO GOZZANO *Alcina and Other Stories*
GUSTAVE GUICHES *The Modesty of Sodom*
EDWARD HERON-ALLEN *The Complete Shorter Fiction*
EDWARD HERON-ALLEN *Three Ghost-Written Novels*
J.-K. HUYSMANS *The Crowds of Lourdes*
J.-K. HUYSMANS *Knapsacks*
COLIN INSOLE *Valerie and Other Stories*
JUSTIN ISIS *Pleasant Tales II*

JULES JANIN *The Dead Donkey and the Guillotined Woman*
VICTOR JOLY *The Unknown Collaborator and Other Legendary Tales*
GUSTAVE KAHN *The Mad King*
MARIE KRYSINSKA *The Path of Amour*
BERNARD LAZARE *The Mirror of Legends*
BERNARD LAZARE *The Torch-Bearers*
MAURICE LEVEL *The Shadow*
JEAN LORRAIN *Errant Vice*
JEAN LORRAIN *Fards and Poisons*
JEAN LORRAIN *Masks in the Tapestry*
JEAN LORRAIN *Monsieur de Bougrelon and Other Stories*
JEAN LORRAIN *Nightmares of an Ether-Drinker*
JEAN LORRAIN *The Soul-Drinker and Other Decadent Fantasies*
GEORGES DE LYS *An Idyll in Sodom*
GEORGES DE LYS *Penthesilea*
ARTHUR MACHEN *N*
ARTHUR MACHEN *Ornaments in Jade*
CAMILLE MAUCLAIR *The Frail Soul and Other Stories*
CATULLE MENDÈS *Bluebirds*
CATULLE MENDÈS *For Reading in the Bath*
CATULLE MENDÈS *Mephistophela*
ÉPHRAÏM MIKHAËL *Halyartes and Other Poems in Prose*
LUIS DE MIRANDA *Who Killed the Poet?*
OCTAVE MIRBEAU *The Death of Balzac*
CHARLES MORICE *Babels, Balloons and Innocent Eyes*
GABRIEL MOUREY *Monada*
DAMIAN MURPHY *Daughters of Apostasy*
KRISTINE ONG MUSLIM *Butterfly Dream*
OSSIT *Ilse*
CHARLES NODIER *Outlaws and Sorrows*
HERSH DOVID NOMBERG *A Cheerful Soul and Other Stories*
PHILOTHÉE O'NEDDY *The Enchanted Ring*
GEORGES DE PEYREBRUNE *A Decadent Woman*
HÉLÈNE PICARD *Sabbat*
URSULA PFLUG *Down From*
JEAN PRINTEMPS *Whimsical Tales*
RACHILDE *The Princess of Darkness*
JEREMY REED *When a Girl Loves a Girl*
ADOLPHE RETTÉ *Misty Thule*
JEAN RICHEPIN *The Bull-Man and the Grasshopper*
FREDERICK ROLFE (Baron Corvo) *Amico di Sandro*
FREDERICK ROLFE (Baron Corvo) *An Ossuary of the North Lagoon and Other Stories*

ARNAUD RYKNER *The Last Train*
LEOPOLD VON SACHER-MASOCH *The Black Gondola and Other Stories*
MARCEL SCHWOB *The Assassins and Other Stories*
MARCEL SCHWOB *Double Heart*
CHRISTIAN HEINRICH SPIESS *The Dwarf of Westerbourg*
BRIAN STABLEFORD (editor)
   Decadence and Symbolism: A Showcase Anthology
BRIAN STABLEFORD (editor) *The Snuggly Satyricon*
BRIAN STABLEFORD (editor) *The Snuggly Satanicon*
BRIAN STABLEFORD *Spirits of the Vasty Deep*
COUNT ERIC STENBOCK *Love, Sleep & Dreams*
COUNT ERIC STENBOCK *Myrtle, Rue & Cypress*
COUNT ERIC STENBOCK *The Shadow of Death*
COUNT ERIC STENBOCK *Studies of Death*
MONTAGUE SUMMERS *The Bride of Christ and Other Fictions*
MONTAGUE SUMMERS *Six Ghost Stories*
ALICE TÉLOT *The Inn of Tears*
GILBERT-AUGUSTIN THIERRY *The Blonde Tress and The Mask*
GILBERT-AUGUSTIN THIERRY *Reincarnation and Redemption*
TOADHOUSE *Gone Fishing with Samy Rosenstock*
TOADHOUSE *Living and Dying in a Mind Field*
TOADHOUSE *What Makes the Wave Break?*
LÉO TRÉZENIK *The Confession of a Madman*
LÉO TRÉZENIK *Decadent Prose Pieces*
RUGGERO VASARI *Raun*
ILARIE VORONCA *The Confession of a False Soul*
ILARIE VORONCA *The Key to Reality*
JANE DE LA VAUDÈRE *The Demi-Sexes and The Androgynes*
JANE DE LA VAUDÈRE *The Double Star and Other Occult Fantasies*
JANE DE LA VAUDÈRE *The Mystery of Kama and Brahma's Courtesans*
JANE DE LA VAUDÈRE *Three Flowers and The King of Siam's Amazon*
JANE DE LA VAUDÈRE *The Witch of Ecbatana and The Virgin of Israel*
AUGUSTE VILLIERS DE L'ISLE-ADAM *Isis*
RENÉE VIVIEN AND HÉLÈNE DE ZUYLEN DE NYEVELT
   Faustina and Other Stories
RENÉE VIVIEN *Lilith's Legacy*
RENÉE VIVIEN *A Woman Appeared to Me*
ILARIE VORONCA *The Confession of a False Soul*
ILARIE VORONCA *The Key to Reality*
TERESA WILMS MONTT *In the Stillness of Marble*
TERESA WILMS MONTT *S^entimental Doubts*
KAREL VAN DE WOESTIJNE *The Dying Peasant*

www.ingramcontent.com/pod-product-compliance
Lightning Source LLC
Chambersburg PA
CBHW060611080526
44585CB00013B/771